F...

"A soul-baring se... ...tains some of the finest personal ... ...*ublishers Weekly*

"Dubus's essays have the same grace and humanity [as his fiction]. They are descriptive and reflective, elegant and astute, autobiographical without being self-indulgent." — *New York Newsday*

". . . absolutely riveting . . . Dubus's writing is characterized by great dignity, meticulous detail, [and] searingly candid observation."
— JOHN JEROME, *Washington Post Book World*

" . . . the crucial aspect of experience in Dubus's essays is the quest for grace. . . . In the sacramental vision of these essays, a man has found solace, and an artist, strength."
— ROBERT TAYLOR, *Boston Globe*

"Graceful, funny and thoughtful by turns, [these essays] are imbued with a sense that life is something serious, and that our business here is to learn how to live it. . . . He has never written better."
— ANDREA BARRETT, *Cleveland Plain Dealer*

"These essays are personal, sometimes painfully personal. There is a craft in the language as well as in the tone. But this craft is never used to disguise the life being probed here. There is simply a man who is a writer named Andre Dubus."
— LEONARD KRIEGEL, *The New York Times Book Review*

"BROKEN VESSELS is, by its end, an overall victory. And its best essays are more than that; they are lessons for life."
— RICK BASS, *Chicago Tribune*

"BROKEN VESSELS confirms not only Dubus's status as a writer — and if there's justice, it will bring him the readers he deserves — but the power of the telling of our stories."
— STEVE PAUL, *Kansas City Star*

BROKEN VESSELS

Broken Vessels

✠

ANDRE
DUBUS

Introduction by
TOBIAS WOLFF

David R. Godine, Publisher
BOSTON

First published in 1991 by
David R. Godine, Publisher, Inc.
300 Massachusetts Avenue
Boston, Massachusetts 02115

First softcover edition published in 1992
Copyright © 1991 by Andre Dubus

LIBRARY OF CONGRESS CATALOGING-IN-PUBLICATION DATA
Dubus, Andre, 1936–
Broken Vessels : essays / by Andre Dubus. — 1st ed.
p.   cm.
ISBN 0-87923-885-2 (HC)
ISBN 0-87923-948-4 (SC)
1. Dubus, Andre, 1936–   —Biography. 1. Novelists,
American—20th century—Biography. I. Title.
PS3554.U265Z465   1991
813'.54—dc20
[B]   91-6711   CIP

"Out Like a Lamb," "Running," "The End of a Season," "Railroad
Sketches," "Of Robin Hood and Womanhood," "The Judge and
Other Snakes," "On Charon's Wharf," "Selling Stories," and "Mar-
keting" first appeared in *Boston Magazine*; "After Twenty Years," in
North American Review; "Two Ghosts" in *Mid-American Review*; "A
Salute to Mister Yates" and "Lights of the Long Night" in *Black War-
rior Review*; "A Woman in April" in *Gentleman's Quarterly*; "Under the
Lights" in *The Village Voice*; "Intensive Care" in *Indiana Review*;
"Bastille Day" in *Yankee*; "Into the Silence" as the introduction to the
anthology *Into the Silence* published by The Green Street Press; "Bro-
ken Vessels" in a condensed version, in *Special Report*; and "Sketches at
Home," "Breathing," and "Husbands" in *Epoch*.

First softcover printing, 1992
Printed in the United States of America

to Geoffrey Moran and his Grace

I am abidingly grateful to Ann Beattie, E. L. Doctorow, Gail Godwin, John Irving, Stephen King, Tim O'Brien, Jayne Anne Phillips, John Updike, Kurt Vonnegut, and Richard Yates. On five Sunday afternoons in the winter of 1987, they read from their work at the ballroom of the Charles Hotel in Cambridge, Massachusetts, to raise money for me and my family, after I was struck by a car and lost a leg. And I am grateful to all those people who came to the benefit readings and to those who mailed checks to me in the year following my injury, and to Scott Downing and Frieda Arkin. All of this kindness saved me from financially going under, and made me feel, during a very bad time, that I had hundreds of friends I didn't even know.

CONTENTS

Contents

INTRODUCTION

ANDRE DUBUS IS my dear friend, but before he was ever my friend he was one of my masters, in the unwitting way that writers sometimes serve as masters to others. I first encountered his work some eight or nine years ago in a back issue of *Ploughshares,* a story called "Corporal of Artillery." I'd done some time in the military myself, and I was struck by his faithful rendering of that life, and the way the story identified the potential for significant experience in peacetime rather than implying, as most fiction with a military setting does, that important things happen to men only when they are at war.

I bought a copy of *Adultery and Other Choices,* the collection of which "Corporal of Artillery" is a part. I figured if the other stories didn't pan out for me I'd at least have one I liked. But I liked them all. I heard in them a voice I hadn't heard before, honest, strong, direct, yet sensuous and emotionally rich. His writing was at the same time intensely compassionate and morally responsible — two qualities you rarely find in combination and even more rarely in balance, as they were here. And so I became not only an admirer but a student of Dubus's stories, as most serious readers of my acquaintance have come to be.

I should add a word: my own first brush with him was misleading — Dubus is not a "military" writer. A relatively small part of his fiction concerns the uniformed life, and though we can sense his affection for a community at least nominally dedicated to values of brotherhood, loyalty, and courage, his work is also critical of that life, dealing as it does with the evil of men being frozen in a vision of manhood that excludes kindness, warmth, enthusiasm, the admission of need for encouragement and love — that teaches them to despise their humanity.

Dubus's stories are essentially domestic and personal. He is most interested in the complexities of human intimacy, a subject he returns to again and again. He is one of the few fiction writers around who writes well about love — not just about lost love, either, in the moping nostalgic manner, but about love before it is lost, love as it is experienced, in whatever form it takes. He is the only writer who has ever made me feel the love of a teenage boy for God, or the love of a teenage girl for the cigarette she is smoking.

His interest in the different forms love can take is mirrored by his interest in the different forms a story can take. No two stories of his move in the same way. By inclination a realist, he can give fantasy the authority of the real, as he does in "An Afternoon with the Old Man." Though his eyes are trained on the here and now, he can without sacrifice of integrity or plausibility engage a character in conversation with God, as he does at the conclusion of "A Father's Story" — and let us hear God's answer. Though more often than not his stories are based on character, he can write wonderfully from pure event, as he does in "The Doctor," or translate character into the realm of the grotesque as in "The Fat Girl" without ever losing our feeling of connection and sympathy. He writes in different forms, from varying points of view, in a language that magically strikes just the right note for the story being told. He is, as I said, a master.

Now, in *Broken Vessels*, we have a collection of autobiographical essays. I was very curious to read them, both because Andre Dubus wrote them and because of my own grappling with the difficulties of writing as myself after years of working behind a mask. Of course the confessional, "genuine" persona is also a construct of the imagination — every coherent persona is — but it will inevitably take on a different voice and presence than the one we inhabit while telling stories. It has to be that way. We have to stand back from our stories — or seem to — like parents at the edge of a pool, watching our children venture into deep water. If we make ourselves obvious, if we meddle, we destroy their chances of ever floating free. But the personal essay is different; it demands that we jump in with both feet, yelling for all we're worth. It doesn't reward authorial discretion, self-effacement, the arts that conceal art. Nor does it reward any of the civic virtues: tact; polish; reasonableness; noble, throatcatching sentiment; correct posture. There are, to be sure, many such writers, and they do very well for themselves, but I have to say they make me see red. I want to reach in and shake them by the jowls until their wisdom and smoothness and certainty crack wide open.

All this parading on the high road has nothing to do with the real possibility of the personal essay, which is to catch oneself in the act of being human. That means a willingness to surrender for a time our pose of unshakable rectitude, and to admit that we are, despite our best intentions, subject to all manner of doubt and weakness and foolish wanting. It requires self-awareness without self-importance, moral rigor without priggishness, and the courage to hang it all on the line. It's a hard thing to do, and this is exactly what Andre Dubus has done here.

Look at the first essay, "Out Like A Lamb." It recounts a year Dubus spent with his family in a mansion that they rented at a bargain rate in return for keeping an eye on eight pedigreed sheep the owner kept for breeding. They didn't have to feed them; all they had to do was catch them when they escaped from their pen and put them back inside. This happened fairly often. At first it was an amusing diversion; then it became irritating, and worse: "our tackling was angry, and some of us punched her in the jaw as we lay on top of her." The punching became habitual, part of the pursuit. One of them died; cause unknown. Finally all the sheep got out together, and in trying to keep them away from the owner's roses Dubus fired a load of birdshot in their direction. Nothing serious, just a bunch of BBs. Another one died. Luckily, the year ran out before the flock. It isn't, as they say, a pretty story, but it's a darkly funny and truthful account of how violence can come to master even someone who hates it. And in describing the process by which this happens, Dubus ignites a sense of recognition in the reader, a palpable memory of sudden anger in the face of gross, incorrigible stupidity, and the cruelty that such stupidity can produce in us. Dubus turns this experience into a meditation on the relationship of Christ to humanity; up to then, he'd always taken the pastoral parables to mean that as His sheep, "we were sweet and lovable . . . But after a few weeks in that New Hampshire house, I saw that Christ's analogy meant something entirely different. We were stupid helpless brutes, and without constant watching we would foolishly destroy ourselves." This thought is not placed as a precept or lesson, at the end of the piece. It occurs, almost in passing, early on. But it resounds through the whole. And so a story of human impatience becomes an intimation of God's infinite patience with us.

This movement is characteristic of Dubus, and he can do it because for him no leap is required; the quotidian and the spiritual don't exist on different planes, but infuse each other. His is an unapologetically sacramental vision of life in which ordinary things participate in the miraculous, the miraculous in ordinary things. He believes in God, and talks to Him, and doesn't mince words. He believes in ghosts — his encounters with two of them are described here. He is open to mystery, and of all mysteries the one that interests him most is the human potential for transcendence. One of my favorite essays, "Under the Lights," tells of his boyhood job shagging foul balls for a hard-luck Class C baseball team, the Lafayette Brahman Bulls. He wanted to play ball himself, and did well in sandlot games, but whenever the game got official he locked up with self-consciousness. He sought help in baseball novels and manuals of advice, and in one of these, a boys' instruction book by Joe DiMaggio, he came across the opinion that if you stay in Class D or C ball for more than one season, you should get out of professional baseball — *quit*.

Dubus repudiates that advice — that word — by evoking the graceful, courageous play of men who spent all their sporting years on C league teams, and who needed no greater justification for their lives than the heart they put into every swing and throw. He remembers a fifty-year-old pitcher who could still deliver no-hitters, and pitch two games back-to-back and win both of them. He remembers, in closing, an unexpected home run by a notoriously soft hitter: "I see Billy Joe Barrett on the night when his whole body and his whole mind and his whole heart were for one moment in absolute harmony with a speeding baseball and he hit it harder and farther than he could at any other instant in his life. We never saw the ball start its descent, its downward arc to earth. For me, it never has. It is rising white over the lights high above the right field fence, a bright and vanishing sphere of human possibility soaring into the darkness beyond our vision."

This essay, like most of the others, is driven by the conviction that the possibility of freedom and grace, even heroism, abides in every life. It is well that Andre Dubus believes this, and believes it so strongly, because in recent years his own life has required exactly such a faith of him. The last and most powerful section of this book is about the accident that cost him one leg above the knee and the effective use of the other, the failure of his marriage, and his enforced separation from his daughters Cadence and Madeleine, the youngest of his six children. They tell of a body irrevocably broken, and the part of a life that depended on that body irrevocably lost, and the struggle of a spirit to build something new.

The description of the accident makes hard reading for me, because I was with Andre not long before it happened, and I remember almost too well the robust, swaggering pleasure he took in his own dense physical being — his body, like his mind, always itching for something strenuous to do with itself. He had a habit of stopping when he saw people in trouble. On an early morning in July of 1986 he was driving home from Boston and came upon a car blocking the right lane of the highway, its taillights darkened. A woman stood beside it. Her forehead was bloodied. Andre pulled over and walked back to see what had happened. The woman was with her brother, a young man just arrived from Puerto Rico. As Andre was trying to calm them and get them off the road a passing car swerved toward them and struck both the brother and Andre. The brother was killed. Andre came close to dying. He spent months in the hospital, had ten operations, and went home as what he insists on calling "a cripple."

It's an important word, not a flourish of self-pity but an insistence on facing his situation honestly. He is crippled. Polite circumlocutions cannot comprehend the enormity of what he has lost, or the fight that each day has become. There is no whining in these essays; Andre Dubus has the writer's gift of subduing shock and rage and grief by translating them into meticulous observation. The world is a different place when seen from a wheelchair, and he documents that difference with the clarity and detail of an explorer in new terrain.

It's a landscape made up of obstacles and traps. How to get at a glass of water the nurse has put out of reach? How to get in and out of cars? How to shave, how to shower? How to reach the dials on the stove? How to reach the cabinets? How to get things from the back of the refrigerator? How to go to the beach without getting stuck in the sand? What do you do if your car breaks down? How do you ask for things without making every request a statement of disability? (I like his solution to this one: you say, *I wonder if there's any cheese? Does anyone want hot chocolate?*)

The simplest transactions become morally complex. Should you call a nurse for your own needs when you hear someone else crying out in pain? How do you tell a loudmouth in a movie theater to shut up? — "If you confront a man from a wheelchair you're bullying him."

Worst of all, how do you protect your children? Andre had to watch helplessly as his baby daughter crawled toward an exercycle, ignoring all the warnings shouted at her, and put her finger in the sprocket. It severed the last joint.

And you have to develop a different sense of time. In the words of Andre's friend David Mix, who lost a leg in Vietnam: "There comes a time in the life of an amputee when he realizes that everything takes three times as long." So this book, which begins with a description of the folly born of impatience, ends with a picture of the same man learning by necessity a patience almost inhuman.

It is not, strangely, a sad book, though terrible things happen in it. Andre lives, as he always did, in a tight web of sons and daughters and friends, more friends than he ever had before. He celebrates them here, and makes them our friends too. What happened to him did not bring him to despair, or even regret. He would do the same thing again, because he believes that it was the right thing, and because he has the tremendous gift of knowing that he saved the woman's life. He had been hit, as he realized then, and as she herself told his doctor, in the very act of pushing her away from the oncoming car.

Andre has made of his wheelchair a place to see the world more clearly than ever. I was struck again and again by the range of his vision, by its depth and compassion, and by the music in which he gives it voice. "After the physical pain of grief has become, with time, a permanent wound in the soul, a sorrow that will last as long as the body does, after the horrors become nightmares and sudden daylight memories, then comes the transcendent and common bond of human suffering, and with that comes forgiveness, and with forgiveness comes love. . . ."

Tobias Wolff
Syracuse, January 1991

Memory, like love, is an act of imagination, an abandonment and a possession.

SUSAN DODD, *MAMAW*

Part One

Out Like a Lamb

OUR FIRST YEAR in New England we lived in a very old house in southern New Hampshire. The landlord wanted someone to live in it while he was working out of the state, the rent was a hundred dollars a month, the house was furnished, had seven fireplaces (two of them worked), and in the backyard was a swimming pool. There were seventy acres of land, most of it wooded except for a long meadow, hilly enough for sledding. There were also three dogs, eight sheep, and a bed of roses. There was a caretaker too, whom I will call Jim: a man in his early thirties, who lived in town where he did other work and came to the house often to see about the lawn, the pump for the swimming pool, the sheep, and the roses. The landlady wanted the roses there when she came home after the year, and the landlord wanted the sheep. They were eight large ewes, and he bred them.

They were enclosed by a wire fence in a large section of

the meadow. They had a shed there too, where they slept. All we had to do about them was make sure they didn't get through the fence, which finally meant that when they got through, we had to catch them and put them back in the pasture. This was my first encounter with sheep. When I was a boy, sheep had certain meanings: in the Western movies, sheep herders interfered with the hero's cattle; or the villain's ideas about his grazing rights interfered with the hero's struggle to raise his sheep. And Christ had called us his flock, his sheep; there were pictures of him holding a lamb in his arms. His face was tender and loving, and I grew up with a sense of those feelings, of being a source of them: we were sweet and lovable sheep. But after a few weeks in that New Hampshire house, I saw that Christ's analogy meant something entirely different. We were stupid helpless brutes, and without constant watching we would foolishly destroy ourselves.

The sheep did not want to leave their pasture, at least not for long and not to go very far. One would find a hole in the fence, slip out, then circle the pasture, trying to get back in. The others watched her. Someone in our family would shout the alarm, and we'd all go outside to chase her. At first we tried herding the ewe back toward the hole in the fence, standing in the path of this bolting creature, trying to angle her back, as we closed the circle the six of us made, closed it tighter and tighter until she was backed against the fence, and the hole she was trying to find. But she never went back through the hole, never saw it, and all our talking and pointing did no good. Finally we gave up, simply chased her over the lawn, around the swimming pool, under trees and through underbrush until one of us got close enough, dived, and tackled. Then three of us would lift her and drop her over the fence, and we'd get some wire and repair the hole. For a while this was fun, but soon our tackling was angry, and some of us punched her in the jaw as we lay on top of her.

One day in that first summer I looked into the shed and saw one of them lying on her side. The others were grazing in the pasture. Next afternoon she was still lying there; I stood at the fence and looked more closely, saw that her mouth was open, her head at a strange angle. I didn't have to look anyway, because by then her stench was on the breeze. I phoned Jim, and he said next day he'd come out and we'd bury her. That evening her smell was in the air over the swimming pool and, closer to the house, it mingled with the aroma of burning charcoal on the patio. So we took the food inside and after dinner I filled a bucket with solid chlorine we sprinkled in the pool. Out in the dark I went through the pasture gate, trying to see the other sheep under the starlit sky. I imagined them huddled upwind from the smell, sleeping out there until someone came and removed death from their shed. The shed was open at its front, but there was a door at the back leading to a narrow platform. I did not want to go through that door, into a place where in the dark I would be alone. I held my breath, opened the door, and stepped in: then the shed was filled with sound and I released my breath, inhaled again in an instant of terror that was suddenly outrage as I saw the other seven sheep rising quickly from where they had been sleeping, around the dead ewe. They ran through the open front, into the light from the sky. They were looking back at me, over their shoulders, and in the pale light their faces looked abject, looked caught, as if they too knew they were more obscene than all the words I was now screaming at them.

When Jim came next day he brought two cigars and we

5

lit them and went to the shed. She was long dead. We both gagged and turned away, then got an old piece of tarpaulin from his pick-up truck. I had phoned him the night before, after going out there and returning to the kitchen and many beers, and said: Jim, let's burn that thing. We need fire. We need *cleans*ing. He had brought a mixture of motor oil and gasoline, saying the oil would thicken the gasoline, make it burn longer. We went back to the shed and, puffing cigars and averting eyes, we pulled the ewe onto the tarpaulin. We gagged again, left the shed, then went back in and dragged her far into the pasture, covered her with sticks, then dead fallen branches, then larger ones, and soaked them and her, then threw a paper torch: the gasoline-whoosh, the quick crackling of sticks and small branches, the sudden heat on our faces, and thick black smoke. The smoke stayed in the air for two days; she took that long to burn. When the fire died in daylight, I went out with more branches and the oil and gasoline and started a new one. On the first night we could see the low flames from our windows. By the second night she was gone.

"Probably a fox got her," Jim said, that morning of the burning. "Or a wolf."

"No wolves around here."

"Could be. Anyway, a fox. Come through the fence and bit her and she bled to death."

There was no blood on the ground, or in the shed, or on the ewe, but I said nothing; the image of a running fox was a lovely one to have that morning, as we sucked on our cigars.

Neither of us had known how long it would take for the ewe to burn. We buried the next one. This was the following spring. They escaped from their pasture in winter too, and wanted to get back to it, and before we tackled them we slipped and fell a lot, and more of us punched their faces as we lay on top of them in the snow and, when we had the strength, we swung them back and forth, holding their legs — one, two, *three* — and flung them over the fence. In spring the roses bloomed and one night all seven sheep got out. We looked from the dinner table and saw them eating the roses, and tenant-fear hurried us outside, to kick and push and pull at those woolly hulks, to shout: No no not her *roses*. They ran around the lawn while we dived at them, missed them, caught them, pulled them kicking toward the fence, and always they got away. It was a warm night, we were sweating, and we had not finished dinner. We were outnumbered seven to six, and our sixth was four years old. We gave up and went inside to eat. But we kept watching them through the windows.

"They've moved down the lawn."

"Have they?"

"They've left the roses, they're just eating the grass now."

"Except one."

"One?"

"One just went back to the roses."

I went to my den where a twelve gauge double-barreled shotgun hung on the wall. I loaded one barrel with bird shot, stepped outside, and aimed at the rump of the rose-eater. When I fired she stopped eating and looked at me. Then she looked at her rump. Then she started eating again. The other sheep had looked up too, and were grazing now. I put up the gun and went back to the table, muttering about sheep not even having the sense to know when they're being shot at. After dinner, a child said: "Something's wrong with the one you shot."

I looked out the back door. The six grazers were still

eating grass; the rose-eater lay on her side, one hind leg sticking upward. I went to her, and crouched. There was blood at her nostrils, and she was not breathing.

"God damn you, don't you die. Do you hear me?" I stood and kicked her. "Don't you dare die on me, Goddamnit." I kicked her again, and she rolled over.

I phoned Jim.

"I'd better come out," he said.

I waited in the backyard, waited out there with beer and guilt and guesses at how much I was going to owe the landlord for my miscalculation about what a number seven shot would do to such a big animal with all that wool on her flesh. Jim came in his pick-up; his twelve-year-old daughter was with him, and when she climbed down from the cab he held up his hand.

"You better wait here," he said, and she got into the cab again.

He squatted over the ewe, felt her chest, and told me she was dead.

"We'll bury her in the morning," he said. "Might's well get the others back in the pasture. Let's drag this one down by the trees."

We dragged her down the sloping lawn to a small clump of pines. Then he called to his daughter and I called to my family and we caught the others one at a time and dropped them over the fence. Jim found the hole and closed it and went home, and I went inside to explain to children about bird shot and trying to get her away from the roses, and to drink beer with my wife and wonder what we'd tell the landlord and how we would pay him.

Next morning Jim and I dug a grave beside the ewe. The earth was hard, and when we had a hole deep enough for her to fill, we rolled her into it. We covered her with a mound, then Jim said: "Something might dig her up. We can use stones, like they do out west."

We carried large stones from the meadow and woods until the grave was covered.

"I guess I've got a letter to write," I said. "And I guess the next one I write will have to include a check."

"Oh? Why's that?"

I pointed at the grave.

"Oh, no, don't write him a letter, and don't tell it in town either. We're both lucky on this one."

"Lucky?"

"Sure. I was supposed to have them bred this winter, and didn't get around to it. I'll tell him this was the only one that took, and she up and died in childbirth. The lamb too."

1978

RUNNING

A SATURDAY AFTERNOON in late July, the heat wave has broken, and I am running at Lake Kenoza with my friend. We first ran together in 1958 when we were second lieutenants in the Officers' Basic School in Quantico, Virginia: ran in the twilit evenings on a dirt road through woods near the apartments where we lived. We ran then, my friend said, for catharsis: from the classes, from the captains and majors, from the patterns of the days. Now on this July afternoon nineteen years later, married to second wives, we are still running for catharsis: the patterns of our lives are more complex, and the running has become more necessary.

The air is cool and dry, as it was Friday, the day after the heat wave broke. That afternoon my wife and her two children and I went to Seabrook beach. I wanted to see the deep blue color the ocean has when the air is dry. The wind and current were strong, from the north. The wind blew sand that stung our flesh, and finally the children wrapped themselves in towels, their faces covered too, looking, to me, like victims of something unspeakable. I lay upwind from my wife and folded a small foam mattress between us, bundling, to shield her small body from the sand. I loved the sun on my flesh, and told my wife I wished I could work at night and sleep on the beach by day, for then I would be free of the night terrors.

At Lake Kenoza on Saturday, the dry air gave the pond and the lake a deeper blue, and the evergreens and leaves were brighter green. Kenoza is on Route 110, going east out of Haverhill, toward the sea. The city tennis courts are there. Across the road from the courts is a pond, and purple loosestrife grows in the marshy earth alongside it. Some people fish there, from the bank. A wide finger of wooded ground separates the pond from the lake. It is a reservoir, so its large surface is free of boats, of swimmers, of fishermen. Mallards and Canadian geese stop here. The best run at Kenoza is five and a half miles, starting at the tennis courts, the road turning left around the pond and into the woods, past the finger of land before the lake, then it curves to the right, following the lake, and as you run you can look to your left at the water, on windy days hear it lapping at the bank, and you can look to your right at the woods. The road leaves the lake only once, going deeper into the woods, toward the hill. As it approaches the hill, there is a second road that goes to the left, down toward the lake again, where the bank drops sharply, and the slope to the right is steep and pine-grown, and brown needles cover it.

This lower road joins one which goes up the hill, a long, curving, deceptive climb; it looks gentle but it is not; a crest appears, you reach it, and look ahead at another one. This is the part of the run where the legs always hurt, the heart pounds, the breathing is hardest. My oldest son ran it with me for the first time three years ago, when he was fourteen; going up the hill he stopped sweating, his face turned red, and I told him he should stop but he shook his head no. I believed he should stop, hoped he would not, remembered first aid I had learned years ago. We reached the top, where the blackberries grow. Another time he ran with me, wearing shoes that were too small. Within the first mile he said the tops of his toes hurt. We slowed the pace, and I urged him to keep going. When I drove him home, he took off his shoes: all his toes were scraped raw on top, bleeding. Later I told that story to a writing student whose novel was beating her. After she had given up on the novel, had her head shrunk out west, and was trying to believe she could live peacefully without daily combat, she wrote to me and said maybe your son should have stopped running. This was before he ran cross-country, then read *Pumping Iron* and accumulated weights, a series of exercises, girth, strength, a new walk, defined muscles, and an identification card for Massachusetts General Hospital where now a specialist tries to cure his injured back. After the crest of the hill, the road goes down again to the lake; the run back to the tennis courts is two and a quarter miles, the water on the right now, the sloping woods on the left, until you leave the shade and run on the open road past the purple loosestrife, the pond, to the tennis players, the parked car, the drive home through the city.

On this Saturday in late July I am not running the hill. I am running one mile, recovering from the west coast of Mexico and two weeks of Montezuma's revenge. ("The last thing I ate before it hit me was fish," I tell Doctor Harbilas in Haverhill. "Ha," he says, "I've been there. It could be somebody breathed on you. It could be *you* breathed.") On the porch of the shed by the courts, young men have finished playing tennis and are listening to the Red Sox game on a transistor radio. My friend and I start running, and he tells me what happened to him two days ago, hiking Mount Washington with his seventeen-year-old daughter. After a mile I turn back and walk, while he runs on. A family is walking behind me. A young couple approaches me, passes on: she has long blonde hair, and they have about them an intimate, furtive look. Once a friend of mine was running up the hill; he looked down toward the lake, saw a boy and girl making love on a large rock; an epiphany, he said, which cheered him the rest of the way. Two young men come up the road; they are wearing shirts and slacks, dull grays and blues, and their faces remind me of young men in the fifties, on their day off from indoor jobs leading nowhere. One of them carries a transistor; they are listening to the ball game. I run back to the tennis courts. The fans on the porch have gone, and I turn on the car radio and listen to the game while I stand waiting for my friend.

Two days earlier he had hiked with his daughter past a sign warning them that Mount Washington has the worst weather in North America, that at any sign of a storm, even in summer, they should turn back. The sky was clear, and they went on; joked, he said, about the warning; cursed it, and climbed. Under a clear sky until they reached the top and saw black clouds coming in fast as blowing dust; then it was raining and hailing. They began walking fast down the road. Then the lightning started. It was not, he said, a scribble across a distant sky. It was starting there, behind them, and on their flanks. Not in front of us, he said; thank God, not in front of us. They started running down the road. He believed he would die, he believed his daughter would die, he thought of what to do if she were struck, father-mouth covering hers, breathing. She looked straight ahead, and down, so she wouldn't see the lightning she heard and felt around her. Running down a curve, they came to a car halted on the way up the mountain. She went to the window and knocked and shouted please let us in out of the lightning.

They were a family from Brooklyn: two children, about ten and twelve, in the back seat; the wife was younger than the husband, and the husband was terrified. I'm not a good driver, he said. Daddy's not a good driver, one of the children said. The children were frightened and, with their father, gentle. My friend's daughter said: My father's a good driver, he can get us down the mountain. The other father got into the back seat with his children. My friend and his daughter got in front, the wife between them, and he turned the car around. I'm not a good driver, the father said. Everything will be all right, the wife said. Everything will be all right, the father said. He'll get us down the mountain, she said. He'll get us down the mountain, the father said.

That Saturday night, after running at Kenoza, I couldn't sleep. I swallowed the pill that wouldn't work and prowled the house, prowled with the nameless terrors until my wife woke up sick at the old dread three in the morning, and she needed me to go downstairs and see if her children had it too, for they had gone to bed with stomach cramps, and I told her their foreheads were cool and they were sound asleep, and then she needed me to hold her while she hurt and I held her and stroked her hair and talked to her and thought if they are sick, tomorrow I'll take care of them, and then I slept. In the morning they were all well.

1977

Under the Lights

for Philip

THE FIRST PROFESSIONAL baseball players I watched and loved were in the Class C Evangeline League, which came to our town in the form of the Lafayette Brahman Bulls. The club's owner raised these hump-backed animals. The league comprised teams from other small towns in Louisiana, and Baton Rouge, the capital. The Baton Rouge team was called the Red Sticks. This was in 1948, and I was eleven years old. At the Lafayette municipal golf course, my father sometimes played golf with Harry Strohm, the player-manager of the Bulls. Strohm was a shortstop. He seemed very old to me and, for a ballplayer, he was: a wiry deeply tanned greying man with lovely blue eyes that were gentle and merry, as his lined face was.

Mrs. Strohm worked in the team's business office; she was a golfer too, and her face was tan and lined and she had warm grey-blue eyes with crinkles at their corners. In the Bulls' second season, she hired me and my cousin Jimmy

15

Burke and our friend Carroll Ritchie as ball boys. The club could not afford to lose baseballs, and the business manager took them from fans who caught fouls in the seats. No one on the club could afford much; the players got around six hundred dollars for a season, and when one of them hit a home run the fans passed a hat for him. During batting practice we boys stood on the outside of the fence and returned balls hit over it, or fouled behind the stands. At game time a black boy we never met appeared and worked on the right field fence; one of us perched on the left, another of us stood in the parking lot behind the grandstands, and the third had the night off and a free seat in the park. Our pay was a dollar a night. It remains the best job I ever had, but I would have to be twelve and thirteen and fourteen to continue loving it.

One late afternoon I sat in the stands with the players who were relaxing in their street clothes before pre-game practice. A young outfielder was joking with his teammates, showing them a condom from his wallet. The condom in his hand chilled me with disgust at the filth of screwing, or doing it, which was a shameful act performed by dogs, bad girls, and thrice by my parents to make my sisters and me; and chilled me too with the awful solemnity of mortal sin: that season, the outfielder was dating a young Catholic woman, who later would go to Lourdes for an incurable illness; she lived in my neighborhood. Now, recalling what a foolish boy the outfielder was, I do not believe the woman graced him with her loins any more than baseball did, but that afternoon I was only confused and frightened, a boy who had opened the wrong door, the wrong drawer.

Then I looked at Harry Strohm. He was watching the outfielder, and his eyes were measuring and cold. Then with my own eyes I saw the outfielder's career as a ball-player. He did not have one. That was in Harry's eyes, and his judgment had nothing, of course, to do with the con-dom: it was the outfielder's cheerful haplessness, sitting in the sun, with no manhood in him, none of the drive and concentration and absolute seriousness a ballplayer must have. This was not a professional relaxing before losing himself in the long hard moment-by-moment work of play-ing baseball. This was a youth with little talent, enough to hit over .300 in Class C, and catch fly balls that most men could not, and throw them back to the infield or to home plate. But his talent was not what Harry was staring at. It was his lack of regret, his lack of retrospection, this young outfielder drifting in and, very soon, out of the profession that still held Harry, still demanded of him, still excited him. Harry was probably forty, maybe more, and his brain helped his legs cover the ground of a shortstop. He knew where to play the hitters.

My mother and father and I went to most home games, and some nights in the off-season we ate dinner at Poor-boy's Restaurant with Harry and his wife. One of those nights, while everyone but my mother and me was smok-ing Lucky Strikes after dinner, my father said to Harry: My son says he wants to be a ballplayer. Harry turned his bright eyes on me, and looked through my eyes and into the secret self, or selves, I believed I hid from everyone, especially my parents and, most of all, my father: those de-mons of failure that were my solitary torment. I will never forget those moments in the restaurant when I felt Harry's eyes, looking as they had when he stared at the young out-fielder who, bawdy and jocular, had not seen them, had not felt them.

I was a child, with a child's solipsistic reaction to the

world. Earlier that season, on a morning before a night game, the Bulls hosted a baseball clinic for young boys. My friends and I went to it, driven by one of our mothers. That was before seatbelts and other sanity, when you put as many children into a car as it could hold, then locked the doors to keep them closed against the pressure of bodies. By then I had taught myself to field ground and fly balls, and to bat. Among my classmates at school, I was a sissy, because I was a poor athlete. Decades later I realized I was a poor athlete at school because I was shy, and every public act — like standing at the plate, waiting to swing at a softball — became disproportionate. Proportion is all; and, in sports at school, I lost it by surrendering to the awful significance of my self-consciousness. Shyness has a strange element of narcissism, a belief that how we look, how we perform, is truly important to other people.

In the fall of 1947 I vowed — I used that word — to redeem myself in softball season in the spring. I used the word *redeem* too. We had moved to a new neighborhood that year, and we had an odd house, two-storied and brick, built alone by its owner, our landlord. It had the only basement in Lafayette, with a steep driveway just wide enough for a car and a few spare inches on either side of it, just enough to make a driver hold his breath, glancing at the concrete walls rising beside the climbing or descending car. The back wall of the living room, and my sisters' shared bedroom above it, had no windows. So I practiced there, throwing a baseball against my sisters' wall for flies, and against the living room wall for grounders. In that neighborhood I had new friends and, since they did not know me as a sissy, I did not become one. In autumn and winter we played tackle football, wearing helmets and shoulder pads; when we weren't doing that, I was practicing baseball.

Every night, before kneeling to say the rosary then going to bed, I practiced batting. I had learned the stance and stride and swing from reading John R. Tunis's baseball novels, and from *Babe Ruth Comics,* which I subscribed to and which, in every issue, had a page of instructions in one of the elements of baseball. I opened my bedroom door so the latch faced me, as a pitcher would. The latch became the ball and I stood close enough to hit it, my feet comfortably spread, my elbows away from my chest, my wrists cocked, and the bat held high. Then one hundred times I stepped toward the latch, the fastball, the curve, and kept my eyes on it and swung the bat, stopping it just short of contact.

In the spring of 1948, in the first softball game during the afternoon hour of physical education in the dusty schoolyard, the two captains chose teams and, as always, they chose other boys until only two of us remained. I batted last, and first came to the plate with two or three runners on base, and while my teammates urged me to try for a walk, and the players on the field called Easy out, Easy out, I watched the softball coming in waist-high, and stepped and swung, and hit it over the right fielder's head for a double. My next time at bat I tripled to center. From then on I brought my glove to school, hanging from a handlebar.

That summer the Bulls came to town, and we boys in the neighborhood played baseball every morning, on a lot owned by the father of one of our friends. Mr. Gossen mowed the field, built a backstop, and erected foul poles down the left and right field foul lines. Beyond them and the rest of the outfield was tall grass. We wore baseball shoes and caps, chewed bubble gum and spat, and at the wooden home plate we knocked dirt from our spikes. We did not have catcher's equipment, only a mask and a mitt, so our pitchers did not throw hard. We did not want them to anyway. But sometimes we played a team from another neighborhood and our catcher used their shin guards and chest protector, and we hit fast balls and roundhouse curves. I don't know about my other friends, but if Little League ball had existed then I would not have played: not with adult coaches and watching parents taking from me my excitement, my happiness while playing or practicing, and returning me to the tense muscles and cool stomach and clumsy hands and feet of self-consciousness. I am grateful that I was given those lovely summer days until we boys grew older and, since none of us was a varsity athlete, we turned to driving lessons and romance.

There were three or four of those baseball seasons. In that first one, in 1948, we went one morning to the Bulls' clinic. The ball field was a crowd of boys, young ones like us, eleven or twelve, and teenagers too. The day began with short drills and instruction and demonstrations; I don't remember how it ended. I only remember the first drill: a column of us in the infield, and one of the Bulls tossing a ground ball to the first boy, then the next boy, and so on: a fast, smooth exercise. But waiting in line, among all those strangers, not only boys but men too, professional ballplayers, I lost my months of backyard practice, my redemption on the softball field at school and the praise from my classmates that followed it, lost the mornings with my friends on our field. When my turn came I trotted toward the softly bouncing ball, crouched, took my eyes off the ball and saw only the blankness of my secret self, and the ball went between and through my legs. The player tossed me another one, which I fielded while my rump puckered as in anticipation of a spanking, a first day at school. Harry Strohm was watching.

So later that summer, amid the aroma of coffee and to-bacco smoke at the table at Poorboy's, when he gazed at me with those eyes like embedded gems, brilliant and ancient, I saw in them myself that morning, bound by the strings of my fear, as the ball bounced over my stiffly waiting gloved hand. Harry Strohm said nothing at the table; or, if he did, I heard it as nothing. Perhaps he said quietly: That's good.

I was wrong, and I did not know I was wrong until this very moment, as I write this. When Harry looked at me across the table, he was not looking at my body and into my soul and deciding I would never be a ballplayer, he was not focusing on my trifling error on that long day of the clinic. He was looking at my young hope and seeing his own that had propelled him into and kept him in this vocation, this game he had played nearly all his life. His skin was deeply, smoothly brown; the wrinkles in his face delineated his skin's toughness. He wore a short-sleeved shirt and slacks. I cannot imagine him in a suit and tie, save in his casket; cannot imagine him in any clothing but a baseball uniform, or something familiar, something placed in a locker before a game, withdrawn from it after the game and the shower, some assembly of cotton whose only function was to cover his nakedness until the next game, the next season. He had once played Triple A ball.

So had Norm Litzinger, our left fielder. A shoulder in-jury was the catalyst for his descent from the top of the wall surrounding the garden where the very few played major league baseball. I do not remember the effect of the injury on his performance in the Evangeline League. Perhaps there was none, as he threw on smaller fields, to hold or put out slower runners, and as he swung at pitches that most major leaguers could hit at will. He was brown, and broad of shoulder and chest, handsome and spirited, and humorous. He was fast too, and graceful, and sometimes, after making a shoestring catch, he somersaulted to his feet, holding the ball high in his glove. Once, as he was sprinting home from third, the catcher blocked the plate. Litzinger ducked his head and ran into the catcher, who dropped the ball as the two men fell; then Litzinger rose from the tumble and dust, grinning, holding his shoulders sloped and his arms bent and hanging like an ape's, and walked like one into applause and the dugout.

He was in his thirties. At the end of every season he went home, to whatever place in the North. For us, everything but Arkansas above us was the North; everything but California, which was isolate and odd. One season he dated a beautiful woman who sat with another beautiful woman in a box seat behind home plate. I was thirteen or fourteen. Litzinger's lady had black hair and dark skin, her lips and fingernails were bright red, her cheeks rouged. Her friend was blonde, with very red lips and nails. They both smoked Chesterfields, and as I watched them drawing on their cigarettes, marking them with lipstick, and blowing plumes of smoke into the humid and floodlit night air, and daintily removing bits of tobacco from their tongues, I felt the magical and frightening mystery of their flesh. The brunette married Norman Litzinger; and one night, before the game, the blonde married Billy Joe Barrett with a ceremony at home plate.

One season I read a book by Joe DiMaggio. I believe it was a book of instruction, for boys. I only remember one line from that book, and I paraphrase it: If you stay in Class D or C ball for more than one season, unless you have been injured, you should get out of professional baseball. Perhaps DiMaggio wrote the word *quit*. I can't. I've spent too much of my life in angry dread of that word.

How could I forget DiMaggio's sentence? I loved young ballplayers who, with the Bulls, were trying to rise through the minor leagues, to the garden of the elect. I loved young ballplayers who, like the outfielder with the condom, were in their second or third seasons in Class C ball. And I loved old ballplayers, like Harry Strohm; and Bill Thomas, a fifty-year-old pitcher with great control, and an assortment of soft breaking balls, who one night pitched a no-hitter; and once, when because of rain-outs and doubleheaders, the Bulls had no one to pitch the second game of a double header, he pitched and won both of them. And I loved players who were neither old nor young, for baseball: men like Tom Spears, a pitcher in his mid-twenties, who had played in leagues higher than Class C, then pitched a few seasons for us on his way out of professional baseball. He was a gentle and witty man, and one morning, because we asked him to, he came to one of our games, to watch us play.

Late one afternoon Mrs. Strohm gave both my cousin Jimmy and me the night off, and we asked the visiting manager if we could be his batboys. Tom Spears pitched for the Bulls that night. This was a time in baseball when, if a man was pitching a no-hitter, no one spoke about it. Radio announcers hinted, in their various ways. Fans in seats looked at each other, winked, raised an eyebrow, nodded. We were afraid of jinxing it; and that belief made being a fan something deeper than watching a game. An uninformed spectator, a drunk, even a thirteen-year-old boy could, by simply saying the words *no-hitter*, destroy it. So you were connected with everyone watching the game, and everyone listening to it too, for a man alone with his radio in his living room, a man who lacked belief, could say those two sacred words and break the spell.

But Jimmy and I did not know until the night Spears pitched a no-hitter, while we were batboys for the New Iberia Pelicans, that the opposing team transcended their desire to win, and each player his desire to perform, to hit, and instead obeyed the rules of the ritual. We were having fun, and we were also trying to do perfect work as batboys; we did not know Spears was pitching a no-hitter. We sat in the dugout while the Pelicans were in the field, sat with pitchers and the manager and reserve ballplayers. When the Pelicans were at bat we stayed close to the on-deck circle, watched hitter after hitter returning to the dugout without a hit. And no one said a word. Then the last batter struck out on a fastball, a lovely glint of white, and the crowd was standing and cheering and passing the hat, and the Bulls in the field and from the dugout were running to the mound, to Spears. Then the Pelicans were saying the two words, surrounding them with the obscenities I first heard and learned from ballplayers, and they went quickly to their bus — there were no visiting locker rooms in the league — and left their bats. Jimmy and I thrust them into the canvas bat bag and ran, both of us holding the bag, to the parking lot, to the bus. The driver, a player, had already started it; the team was aboard. Your bats, we called; Your bats. From the bus we heard the two words, the obscenities; a player reached down through the door and hoisted in the bag of Louisville Sluggers.

How could I forget DiMaggio's sentence? Our first baseman, in the Bulls' first season, was a young hard-hitting lefthander whose last name was Glenn. We were in the Detroit Tiger system, and after Glenn's season with us, he went up to Flint, Michigan, to a Class A league. I subscribed to *The Sporting News* and read the weekly statistics and box scores, and I followed Glenn's performance, and I shared his hope, and waited for the season when he would stand finally in the garden. At Flint he batted in the middle of the order, as he had for us, and he did well; but he did not hit .300, or thirty home runs. In the next season I looked every week at the names in *The Sporting News*, searched for Glenn in double A and triple A, and did not find him there, or in Class A or B, and I never saw his name again. It was as though he had come into my life, then left me and died, but I did not have the words then for what I felt in my heart. I could only say to my friends: I can't find Glenn's name anymore.

I believed Billy Joe Barrett's name would be part of baseball for years. I believed he would go from us to Flint, then to double and finally triple A, and would have a career there, at the top of the garden wall. And, with the hope that is the essence of belief, I told myself that he would play in the major leagues; that one season, or over several of them, he would discover and claim that instant of timing, or that sharper concentration, or whatever it was that he so slightly lacked, and that flawed his harmony at the plate. In the field he was what we called then a Fancy Dan. He was right-handed and tall, fast and graceful and lithe. He leaped high and caught line drives as smoothly as an acrobat, as though the hard-hit ball and his catching it were a performance he and the batter had practiced for years. On very close plays at first, stretching for a throw from an infielder, he did a split, the bottom of one leg and the top of the other pressed against the earth; then quickly and smoothly, without using his hands, he stood. He stole a lot of bases. He often ended his slide by rising to his feet, on the bag. He batted left-handed and was a line drive hitter, and a good one; but not a great one.

I have never seen a first baseman whose grace thrilled me

as Barrett's did; and one night in Lafayette he hit a baseball in a way I have never seen again. He batted lead-off or second and every season hit a few home runs, but they were not what we or other teams and fans or Barrett himself considered either a hope or a threat when he was at the plate. But that night he hit a fast ball coming just above his knees. It started as a line drive over the second baseman, who leaped for it, his gloved hand reaching up then arcing down without the ball that had cleared by inches, maybe twelve of them, the glove's leather fingers. Then in short right field the ball's trajectory sharply rose, as though deflected higher and faster by angled air, and the right fielder stopped his motion toward it and simply stood and watched while the ball rose higher and higher and was still rising and tiny as it went over the lights in right field. Billy Joe Barrett's career ended in Lafayette.

How could I forget DiMaggio's sentence? Before I got out of high school, the Bulls' park was vacant, its playing field growing weeds. The Strohms had moved on, looking for another ball club; and Norm Litzinger and Billy Joe Barrett and their wives had gone to whatever places they found, after Lafayette, and after baseball. I was driving my family's old Chevrolet and smoking Lucky Strikes and falling in love with girls whose red lips marked their cigarettes and who, with painted fingernails, removed bits of tobacco from their tongues; and, with that immortal vision of mortality that youth holds in its heart, I waited for manhood.

DiMaggio was wrong. I know that now, over forty years after I read his sentence. Or, because I was a boy whose hope was to be a different boy with a new body growing tall and fast and graceful and strong, a boy who one morning would wake, by some miracle of desire, in motion on the path to the garden, I gave to DiMaggio too much credence;

and his sentence lost, for me, all proportion, and insidiously became a heresy. Which I am renouncing now, as I see Billy Joe Barrett on the night when his whole body and his whole mind and his whole heart were for one moment in absolute harmony with a speeding baseball and he hit it harder and farther than he could at any other instant in his life. We never saw the ball start its descent, its downward arc to earth. For me, it never has. It is rising white over the lights high above the right field fence, a bright and vanishing sphere of human possibility soaring into the darkness beyond our vision.

1989

THE END OF A SEASON

O N   A   S U M M E R Wednesday they came in, the carpenter and the plumber, to install a shower. The plumber is short and white-haired, the carpenter tall and white-haired. In winter the plumber had gone to Texas, to a job that was waiting. It was his first move from New England. When he got there the job wasn't, so he came back to work for the college.

"Thought I'd got rid of you," the carpenter said. He was standing in the bathtub. "Then I goes to work one morning, and there's that Goddamn plumber."

"I missed you," the plumber said.

"I bet you did. You'll miss me when I'm gone too."

"You going somewhere?" I said.

"You bet I'm going somewhere," the carpenter said.

"Happy hunting ground," the plumber said. "That's where he's going."

The carpenter planned to finish his work on Friday, and

the plumber his on Monday, but the parts didn't come that week. Monday morning the carpenter came up the stairs, three flights of them. He went into the bathroom and started working.

"Damndest thing about that plumber," he said. "I come to work Friday and all day I'm looking around for him. Where's that plumber? I say. Nobody's seen him. So I figure he's working down to the other end, or something. So I come in this morning, and no plumber. Where's that plumber? I say. Turns out he had a heart attack. He's in the hospital. Last week he's climbing these stairs and puffing and he says, *Jes*us I got to quit them Goddamn cigarettes. Sure, I say, you and me both. Thursday he's at lunch and his arm goes numb but he works the rest of the afternoon anyways, then I guess that night his wife got him down to the hospital. I guess he'll quit the butts now."

"Maybe. Most people don't."

"That's true. But you put a guy in the hospital for a while, he's feeling sick, he don't *want* to smoke; then after a while he goes home and he can quit. When it's gradual like that. It's cold turkey that guys can't do."

"My father had a heart attack. Next day I went to see him, he was in the oxygen tent, and I said: Is there anything you want? He said: A highball and a cigarette."

"Fix him right up."

"Sure. They told him to quit, so he switched from Luckies to Marlboros."

"Jesus, them's worse. That's what *I* smoke. So is he all right now?"

"No, he died. Cancer of the colon."

"No fooling. They get you one way or the other, don't they?"

————

I went to the college and talked to a woman who cleans the place.

"How's Art?" I said.

"You mean Merton," she said.

Merton was her husband. He used to clean the place too, but then he had a heart attack. They told him he couldn't smoke anymore; he was a Red Sox fan, and they told him he couldn't watch the games on television either, he'd get too excited.

"I mean the plumber." I said. "He had a heart attack last week."

"Oh my Gawd. I'll call his wife."

"How you going to keep your man away from the tube, with the Yankees playing?"

"Oh, that poor man: he watched maybe one or two innings this weekend, with Seattle. I just go with what I got, one day at a time."

A few days later, Merton was in the college bookstore, talking with the woman who runs it. He was short, and very thin.

"I can't even eat bread," he said to her.

"You should try that salt-free bread."

"You ever taste bread without salt in it?"

"I hear you can't watch the games," I said.

"Sure. The doctor said, you've got a weak heart, you can't watch baseball; I said, yeah, well you've got a weak head, and I'm watching the Sox." He grinned at the woman. "It's crazy: every time I hear a knock on the door I figure it's St. Peter come calling."

"Oh, you," she said.

"I tell you, when I find out I'm going down the Glory

Road I'm buying me a case of beer and a carton of cigarettes."

"Oh, I'm not even going to listen to you," she said, and she squeezed his hand on the counter between them.

Within a week he was dead. The day before his funeral I ran across the campus. The carpenter was working on the footbridge over the pond, and I stopped. He said the plumber had angina and had to stay home and rest.

"Old Merton's getting himself buried out in the boondocks," he said.

"I don't know where it is."

"Me neither. Kenny'll know."

We went to the other end of the bridge where Kenny was clipping brush. He told us where the cemetery was.

"Kenny's bought his plot already," the carpenter said. "Tombstone and all."

"The stone too?"

"Sure," Kenny said. "I got it cheap, up in New Hampshire. Went up there in my truck and brought it back."

"And it's out there?" I said. "With your name on it?"

"Is it *out* there," the carpenter said. "Memorial Day, Kenny went and took a look at it. Veterans had it all decorated. They figured he was down there, see."

"Oh, it looked pretty," Kenny said. "Flags, flowers, the whole works."

"You do plan ahead," I said.

"It's the one thing you can count on," Kenny said.

"I'll see you guys later," I said, and ran away from the campus, and down the road.

1978

31

RAILROAD SKETCHES

T RAVEL BY AIR is not travel at all, but simply a change
of location; so my wife and daughter and I went to
San Francisco by train, leaving Boston on a Wednesday
morning in June then, after lunch in New York, boarding
Amtrak's Broadway to Chicago. My daughter had a room-
ette, my wife and I a bedroom: the couch, facing the front
of the train, becomes a bed; above it is a bunk, locked into
the wall, lowered at night; a narrow shoe locker has hangers
for shirts; there is a bathroom with a lavatory latched into
the wall above the toilet; you lower it to wash and when you
lift it into the wall again, it drains; the room has a wide
window and is air-conditioned, and a small fan over the
door stirs the air above the couch, the bunks.

We go to the club car as the train gets underway, and are
sitting with our first drinks when the porter who showed
us aboard comes in and sits at the table across the aisle. He
looks at me and says: "You're in the wrong car."

"This one?"

"No. The bedroom. Room A is right, but it's Room A in the *next* car."

I follow him out and we move the luggage and I go back to my drink and watch the backward rush of late spring green, while a boy with a transistor radio plays rock music so loudly that no table or booth is free of it, and I wonder if we need an amendment to the First Amendment, or thousands of violated Americans willing to break the portable radios of those people whose sonic selfishness disturbs the sound of breakers and breeze at beaches, the quiet of parks, and even the sounds of baseball and fans and vendors at Fenway Park where I've often heard the play-by-play from nearby fans with strange needs, and once heard a basketball game from the row behind me.

My wife asks him to turn it lower and he does, and we pass trees interrupted by parking lots and factories and stores and houses of small towns, and I remember the cities our trains have crept through since morning, where the tall bleak monuments stood, walls of indefinable color, not brown or grey or black: the color of hopes slowly constricted through the years, and I look out at lovely farms and grazing dairy cattle in green pastures in maligned New Jersey. In a light rain we cross the Delaware into Trenton; on the river a man stands in an outboard, under a sheltering bridge. West of Trenton are suburbs, with softball diamonds and supermarkets and pastel houses, small and built close to each other, those little homes where people paid for a piece of the country, and to judge them from the distance of a train, with an eye for size and space, to judge them from anywhere, is foolish; for finally you know that, as with the train compartment, one could disappear nightly and happily into those houses. But somehow they seem sad, perhaps because I believe that anyone who wants to own one of them would also want to own a bigger one with more lawn and trees, so the house becomes another burial place of surrendered hope. Maybe it means that, along the tracks, America is sad.

Philadelphia is the saddest, so far, of all: looking as though it has been defeated after a long siege, ending in house-to-house combat, and then abandoned, leaving the brick factories and mills with their broken windows, and the dwellings built together without yards or even a glimpse of light between them, all these buildings looking vacated months ago by the wounded and dead. But leaving Philadelphia we go through Bryn Mawr where, for a short distance, there is not only light between homes but wide lawns with trees, dark green in the grey light of the wet sky. The hope for a piece of the country is realized here: a piece of it far enough away from neighbors so you cannot smell, hear, or even see them; and again the train's sleeping compartment comes to mind, its sealed-in privacy paid for more dearly than the coach seats, where you smell and hear and see everyone; so that the train becomes a mobile microcosm of the land.

It is cocktail hour in the club car, and the citizenry are reading bad books. I am sipping a vodka and tonic when, not three feet from my window, which is wider than the table where we sit, an eastbound train rushes past, adding to the stimulation of liquor: I feel I can reach out and touch speeding steel. At six o'clock the sun breaks through, trees and meadows are lighter green and, far from the tracks, white houses are nestled at the edge of forested hills. Then we are in farm country: long wide fields east of Lancaster, some separated by trees growing in line; large houses and barns, and the sky here is touched by trees and silos. Now the outskirts of cities are as something seen long ago, memory of them muted by this landscape, and I know I have not lost touch with the land but, reared in towns and suburbs, was already removed from it at birth. People's love of the country is simple and profound: out here one lives on real earth, not a measured and manicured replica of it, or in an apartment whose seclusion consists of steel and concrete rising above the streets, and high up there, one can have colored walls and the smells of toiletry and cooking. We pass trees so dense that we cannot see between them, our vision narrowed to our window and the green trees in the late sunlight, and the sky patched with blue. Then we leave the trees and, in the open, the sky is slashed by tall grey turrets and we pass Three Mile Island. Then we go along the tree-grown banks of the Susquehanna, into Harrisburg. By dinner the sun is out, the sky blue, and as we are seated we cross the Susquehanna, broad, with tiny grassy islands.

The steward comes for our drink orders: a vodka and tonic, and a half bottle of burgundy with two glasses. He assumes the two glasses are for my wife and daughter, and says: "I'll bring it and you pour it. I know they're not twenty-one, and I won't touch it."

I tell him one glass is for me, the other for my young wife. When he brings the wine, he pours it and says: "Pennsylvania, Iowa, Texas, Arkansas are the bad states. We know them. They come aboard and arrest the bartender. In Oklahoma you can only sell beer with an Oklahoma stamp on it."

Still we are following the Susquehanna, trees along the banks, the earth rising in ridges to the horizon. I go to the club car so I can smoke with my drink, and sit with a black man with white hair and moustache. He is from New Jersey, and he and his wife are going to St. Louis to visit a niece.

"I was supposed to be born in New Orleans," he says. "But my daddy got on a moving van and didn't have the sense to get off. He just couldn't stay settled. Started in Georgia, got to Louisiana, ended in Trenton."

"Are you still working?"

"I own a garage, knock out a few dents. Something to do while I'm retired. But it's hard to keep help."

"They don't show?"

"They don't show, or when they do, they want all the money."

He tells me to watch for the horseshoe turn later that night.

"You see a train moving and you think it's another train, then you realize it's the same one you're riding."

"Maybe I'll see you here for that, after dinner."

"Maybe. My wife's up in the car. I came back to smoke. She worries about our stuff, wants to watch it all the time. I try not to worry. This year I'll be seventy-two. How much can I take with me?"

"Six feet of the country."

"They probably won't give me all of that."

I go back to the dining car; the sun is setting behind trees, peering through as though perched on the fork of bough and trunk; then it is on the crest of a blue ridge, beyond the river and trees.

After dinner I drink a beer in the club car and talk with Doris, a black woman tending bar. She asks where I am going, then says: "You'll love the Zephyr: two decks, and the scenery from Denver on west is beautiful. My husband is a retired veteran, and he flew a lot in the service, but

36

hadn't hardly been on trains. So we were going to L.A. and I said Let's go by train. He fell in *love* with it. He loved it so much that he took the train *back* from L.A. I'm telling you, honey, he left before me, and I *flew* back."

"You married an older man too. You don't look over twenty-five."

"I'm past twenty-five, but my husband's *forty*-five."

"My wife's twenty-three."

"There you go. Nothing wrong with that. I'd never marry a young man again: too many *has*sles. You got to get somebody *sett*led. This man that works for Amtrak asked me about a *friend* of his that was forty-seven and wanted to marry a girl that was twenty. But I knew he was talking about himself. I told him: Listen: don't worry about age. It don't mean nothing. You need a woman that understands your work and loves you. Some can and some can't and don't matter how old they are. He said he wanted some children. I said Go ahead and *have* children. Then he said he was worried because she was going to go to *col*lege. I said She's not worried about you *not* having an education, so don't worry about her *hav*ing one."

We sleep in Pennsylvania with the shade up so we can watch the darkness and street lights and silhouettes of trees. I wake at five-thirty in sunlight and the flat green country east of Fort Wayne: farms, the neighborhoods of white houses looking less desperate, more sturdy that those east of us, crouching at the sides of cities, like sleeping rabbits in the shadow of the hawk. I wonder if politicians know less about the land, now that they campaign by air. From the tracks, Fort Wayne is attractive. Under a light blue sky streaked with cirrus clouds, the city's few tall buildings are pale beige. The streets are wide and quiet, probably looking

wide because they are quiet. The houses near the tracks are
old; many of them are two-storied, and in their lawns are
old trees. Leaving these, as I order poached eggs on corned
beef hash, we move through wooded country, then farms
again and country neighborhoods, the houses spaced
among low hills and clustered trees.

At Chicago the train passes homes where blacks live: at
first they are decently spaced, single-story, with yards and
trees, much like the white suburbs outside other cities, but
juxtaposed with vacant weed-grown lots and junkyards;
farther on, the houses become four- or five-storied tene-
ments with less and less space between them until, in the
final area before the train yard, there is none. It is strange
to come into a city after the expanse of country, and I feel
I am looking at pictures of my country's history: a city built
because of a lake, and on the city's outskirts the blacks,
descended from slaves, cheap labor pushed northward,
holding their piece of the land — the few rooms, the
screened windows — under the concrete-pierced sky.

We are in Chicago at nine-thirty and spend the day in the
city with a friend, showers and a change of clothes, mar-
garitas and Mexican food at *la Margarita;* we walk to book-
stores on Michigan Avenue and buy Simenon, Zola, James
Webb, and Sara Vogan. We leave at six-fifty that evening
on the San Francisco Zephyr, with a family room for the
three of us: the couch becomes a double bed and there is a
fold-down bunk above it and another at its foot; a few paces
away, down the hall, are six good bathrooms. We are on the
first floor. Before dinner we go to the second floor club car,
with wide windows and overhead windows, swivel chairs
and couches, and we go through green farm country under
the enormous circus tent of the midwestern sky, the sun
descending, an orange ball over trees and rooftops, a long

grey-blue cirrus cloud at the horizon, almost the color of a distant ship; then, the sun gone, a strip of gold cloud and trees silhouetted against the rose and golden sky, their crowns burnished, and we go with that sunset for miles, then into the night.

On Friday we wake in Nebraska, and I think about the blacks: the porters and stewards, bartenders and waiters, each of them with a certain *duende,* so that, like the porter leaving New York ("You're in the wrong room"), they are friendly in a way that lets you know they are not paid attendants, servile to the whim of anyone owning a ticket, but your proud and sometimes avuncular hosts. Perhaps this comes from knowing the train so well, from the cama- raderie of work, from the skillful legs and hands that don't stumble or spill, from feeling finally that it's *their* train; and it occurs to me that this is good work for the dispossessed of the land: seeing the country's landscapes from a clean mobile home and place of work, a place they know and command, as if The Man Without a Country had been given command of a ship to cruise America's coasts and rivers.

At breakfast we enter Colorado, the country mostly flat and grassy, with scattered trees and low green scrub brush. The sky is cloudless, an expanse of unbroken blue from horizon to horizon. Cows watch us, and a jackrabbit bolts. After breakfast, the club car is filled, so we go down to our room, which occupies the width of the car, with wide win- dows on both sides. To the north there are ridges as we move toward Denver. West of Fort Morgan we are in roll- ing terrain, some large farms, penned cattle, then grass and white and yellow flowers growing wild. By eleven o'clock we can see the Rockies. Leaving Denver, we skip lunch, sit in the club car, and look out at the snow-capped mountain range to the west, as the train goes north to Cheyenne, where we turn west toward Laramie and see antelopes standing in the open. Because they are so close to the train, they seem tame; but then I realize that there are no people out there, and the train is going through their country, whose flat scrub-grown surface is split by long draws, and rises steeply into buttes and, in the distance, mesas. We stop at Rawlins and I go downstairs, to the bar, to buy cigarettes. A black woman named Sharon Avington is tending bar, selling snacks, and working a microwave oven. She doesn't have Marlboros.

"I've got ex*otic* brands: Merit, Kent III, Salem Lights — but you see those machines in the station?" She points through the open door at a window in the small station. "You go in there. But don't dawdle."

I go, stopping long enough to read the sign on the station door:

> *Rule of the day:* DON'T *get off the train if you*
> *can't hurry back.*
> *Missed this month — 3*
> *Near misses — 0*

In the club car we watch grazing antelope, russet buttes, and the citizenry. While driving the highways and walking the streets and roads of America, I blame the garbage I see on an abstraction: *they* dropped their emptied cigarette packs and cans and bottles and wrappers and boxes. Here on the train we watch them do it. There are no waiters in the club car, but there is a large garbage can; the arms of the chairs and the tables have ashtrays. By mid-afternoon smokers and drinkers have come and gone, leaving behind their coat-of-arms: ashes and cans and plastic glasses. I watch one couple, a man with greying short hair and his wife; their dress and faces appear conservative, and I imagine their kitchen at home: clean, orderly, the emptied can or bottle immediately removed from the table and dropped in the garbage hidden behind a cupboard door. Yet on the table they share between their seats at the window, and in the shallow trough for drinks beneath the window, cans and glasses accumulate, ashes and matchsticks scatter. Then they leave.

First call for dinner is supposed to be at five, but today it is late, and the citizenry are lining up in the club car aisles, muttering behind our chairs as we watch the country. Downstairs Sharon is chilling the champagne we brought. A large woman keeps saying she will write to Amtrak. Others call for the steward. A wiry greying man in his fifties goes into the dining room and comes back with word: We were late getting to Rawlins and they had to turn off the power when we stopped there and the chefs did not want to start cooking before that, and then lose power.

"But he's only a Negro," the wiry man says.

My wife goes downstairs to the bar, comes back with the champagne, and I hold plastic glasses over her lap while she works on the cork. It pops loudly and the large woman softly screams.

"I thought it was a gun," she says.

People laugh nervously, and for a while their anger dissipates. We drink the bottle of champagne while behind us in the aisle the voices rise again, and people sway against the backs of our seats. Outside the land stretches

41

wide and treeless, broken by the steep sides and flat tops of buttes. Then we see a prairie dog village. At some of the holes, prairie dogs stand erectly and watch the passing train.

On Saturday, the last day of the journey, I wake in Carlin, Nevada. We are going through foothills then Battle Mountain, a town of trailers, with a sign at the highway: *The Barite Capitol of the World.* I go upstairs, through sleeping cars and the dining car, the smells of bacon and pancakes coming from the kitchen below, a few people eating early breakfast, through the club car, clean now and empty, and down to the bar. Sharon is working, and while I drink coffee a woman and her daughter, about eight, come in. The girl is barefooted and Sharon tells the woman not to let the child walk barefooted on the train. She says to the girl: "When you grow up and get married your husband will want to kiss your toes, and you want to have all five of them."

Near the tracks, a coyote trots west. My wife comes in for coffee, and Sharon sits with us in a booth; in the booth across the aisle are a couple and their seven-year-old daughter and a boy who belongs to no one in the car, and who wears a T-shirt with, printed across the chest: *Caution: Here Comes Trouble.* Sharon talks to him. He is five, and his name is Casey. He is sitting beside the girl and, now and then, he peers at her and smiles. He and his mother and two-year-old sister are going to Martinez, he says. He keeps striking his left palm with his right fist. After a while, a conductor comes to the foot of the stairs.

"Did you know you've been lost?" he says. "Come on, son." He looks at the girl, and says: "I don't blame him for following *that* pretty girl around."

Casey leaves with him, and the girl says: "I wish that boy took an airplane."

"They lose them all the time," Sharon says. "Soon as they come aboard, they expect the conductors to look after the kids. We had one drunk woman who got off in Omaha and forgot her little boy. A conductor found him curled up asleep in a men's room. So they wrapped him in blankets and left him at the station in Sparks."

"How far is that from Omaha?"

"Five hundred and twenty-two miles. But there wasn't anyplace to leave him in between."

I tell her about the angry people waiting for dinner last night.

"They're just bored," she says. "If they had some dis*trac*tion, they'd be all right. And they're the same ones that've been nickel-diming me all afternoon for snacks."

We talk about Amtrak people losing jobs because of Reagan's budget; and propositions thirteen in California and two and a half in Massachusetts taking away more jobs, and public services as well, and she says: "Those people in power: they make a decision on paper, in their offices. But where's the heart? The heart, that *is* this country."

After breakfast we move southwest along the Truckee River, through the mountains. A huge bird flies over the valley between the tracks and the mountains: dark grey, wide wings, moving up toward the high brown slopes spotted green with scattered brush. Two palominos are drinking in the river; they stand among rocks, the water beneath their knees, and the high country is closing in on the tracks, cutting off and diminishing the blue sky with small puffs of solitary white clouds, and we go to the club car to watch the Sierra Nevadas.

Reno's so close to hell you can see Sparks, a trainman said. In

43

Reno we pass tawdry casinos and hotels, and look away, at the mountains beyond them. Quickly we are past Reno's outskirts, going between hills and past grazing sheep, to California: to Truckee in the Sierra Nevadas which rise now on both sides with slender evergreens growing up their slopes and with green shrubs on the lower hills and grass farther up. A young man and a boy are wading in the smooth-flowing river, fishing for trout. To the north, across the river, high on a bank, is Highway 80, and beyond it the mountains rise steeply, slopes of rock and brush and evergreens. We cross the river, it is south of us now, and I turn my seat around to watch it and the peaks we are leaving. We stop at Truckee, where the buildings are old, made of bricks, brown ones and red ones and one of yellow stone. They are lined facing the tracks on Donner Pass Road: Capitol Saloon and Dance Hall, shops, and on the hills above the road, old wooden houses among the evergreens.

The train climbs and the sun comes into my lap through the overhead window; behind us there is snow on the peaks. We reach Donner Lake, large and surrounded by trees, deep blue in the sunlight and dry air. We are in Donner Pass where they froze and starved, then through a long tunnel, someone's lighter flares in the dark, and we come out in pines where houses are, trees growing thickly between them, the houses of redwood with aluminum roofs shining silver in the sun. We are going gradually down, the highway beneath us now, and beyond it is a narrow valley of trees, then the upward slope of a mountain, with evergreens covering most of it except for a wall of rock and patches of bare earth. The pines are tall and straight and slender, some almost cylindrical until the final tapering at their tops, others the shape of cones. A lone red peak, ridge-shaped, appears behind the peaks to the north of us, across the highway, which is far below now as we pass large rocks, deep gorges and, always, the evergreens. On a red rock near the tracks someone has written in white stones: HELLO.

We go through a short tunnel, come out with cabins below us, aluminum-roofed, a winding dirt road going down the mountain. Slowly we descend, pass south of and above a lake, ringed by brown hills and pines; the power lines in the distance are going downhill like silver ribbons through the trees. Then, between the slope we ride on and the mountain to the north, there is a long green valley stretching west, so that power lines and rails and train and the earth itself, the mountains and valley, are moving toward the sea.

My daughter tells me to look at the organized trees behind me: to the south the pines grow from a draw up the mountain so uniformly that a man from Ireland asks if they were planted, then says: "If you built a house in there, you'd have a bear at your door." I go down to the bar for a beer and when I come up again I look down a ravine and across a deep wooded draw at mountains; the tracks curve and descend through trees and rocks and red earth, and the Irishman says: "I've seen trees in my time, but never like this: as far as the eye can see, and then some."

We leave the mountains and move into rolling country that feels hot through the windows; a cactus grows in a box in a backyard, there are palm trees and apple orchards, and a pasture where cows graze and, among them, a white goat stands motionless on a lone rock. Groups of trailers are parked against palm trunks, under the wide leaves. The country changes to gently rolling land, and between lumber yards and houses, horses graze; we cross a river where a man fishes from a small island, and a man and his black dog ride in an outboard.

Between Roseville and Sacramento the land flattens and is crowded and we have reached, or returned to, cluttered America living close enough to each other to hear and recite the neighbors' quarrels and exclamations of joy and grief, the only spaces those cleared of trees and reserved for sport: softball diamonds and golf courses. I am saddened by what we make: the buildings where they might as well hang a sign: THIS UGLY PLACE IS WHERE YOU WORK, the playing fields and parks, and the house to contain you. While somehow there is a trick at work and you have been removed not only from the land itself, but from its spirit; or, as Sharon says, the heart. After the open country and mountains, the earth looks punished, and it is hard to believe that its people have not been punished as well, for nothing more than the desire to love and to prove oneself worthy of that by going to work.

West of Davis there are irrigated farms and fields of yellow-brown hay with a wide black strip where they have burned it. To the south the sky is broad, nearly midwestern, but it seems lower; to the north it is hazy and broken by a mountain range. Corn is growing. Near us the low hills are grown with hay, and the trees on them are darker green against their sand dune color. Turning southwest we go through a stretch of marsh, white herons rising from it; then rows of grey ships are sitting on green and yellow grass, and we see the wide Sacramento and cross it and from the bridge we see the ships mothballed at Vallejo. We stop at Martinez and watch Casey outside with his mother and two-year-old sister, their hair moving in the breeze, Casey punching his palm with his fist.

Then we go downriver. On the opposite bank are blond hills; then men are fishing from a wharf, there is a marina with sailboats and fishing boats, and we are going south along the Bay. It is wide, muddy near the shore, then green, and across it there are blue ridges against the pale sky. Then we see the Oakland Bridge and, far off, the Golden Gate Bridge, and trees shaped by the wind leaning forever to the east, and a teenage black boy, lean and muscular in his shorts, jogging north along the tracks, his hands high, at his shoulders, punching: hooking and jabbing the sunlit air.

1981

Part Two

Of Robin Hood and Womanhood

W HEN I WAS a graduate student at the University of
Iowa I had a wife and four children, and an income
of about four thousand dollars a year, and I stood in line
monthly for food handed out by the state. My juxtaposition
with the others in line made me uncomfortable, for I was
usually wearing a tie and jacket for my duties as a teaching
assistant, I was in my twenties, and I felt that, to the others
in line, I looked like a man with hope and direction; at the
very least, a man who was only temporarily a part of that
line and the life it helped support. I brought home cans and
cartons of butter, cheese, peanut butter, flour, and chunks
of strange meat reminiscent of C-rations; but with imagination, the meat could be made into a casserole that was more
than merely edible. I also knew, as I stood in line with the
poor, that I had chosen to leave a good salary, had chosen
to go to graduate school, while for those other people the
act of choosing was so limited that it was not, and would

probably never be, an essential part of their lives.

But there was another way I brought home the bacon, a romantic way that could not have been romantic when it was the only way a man could feed the bodies he loved. In the fall we went hunting, my friends and I; sometimes there were so many of us that we resembled a rifle squad walking abreast through the cornfields. None of us went hunting because it was a cheap way to feed families. The money for licenses and shells would have bought more food in a super-market. We hunted because we were friends, and because we loved to hunt: to slip between the cornstalks in autumn and, as winter started, to walk over the snow or frozen earth and the cornstalks lying now stiff as wood; to flush the rabbit and fire over his bounding tail at his head; and, best of all, the sudden rush of the pheasant, the quick shooting, and the always fair decision, in doubtful cases, about whose gun, whose finger and eye, had killed the bird. At the end of those weekend afternoons I brought home the game and placed it on the picnic table where we ate in the kitchen, and I was able to forget what it had actually cost in time and money, to see it simply as lovely meals I had brought home, a supplement to the C-ration casseroles, the spaghetti, the beans and rice. They were meals which even demanded that rarity in the house, a bottle of wine. All of this was a delusion, but it was a good one: gun in hand, looking at a cock pheasant on the table, its feathers bringing to the kitchen the aura of the field, the cold wind, the intensity of the hunt, and the thrilling release of the death shot. I felt I had done what a man should do for his family.

Romance dies hard, because its very nature is to want to live. Forty-one years old and living in 1977, I still have that need to do something pure and clean and male about bread-winning, something to replace or at least supplement the paycheck: for the paycheck seems nothing more than a piece of paper with numbers and my name on it, a paper deposited monthly in my account, its numbers having nothing to do with my work, for I love teaching and so I rarely see the classroom and the salary as having any connection. And the business of paying bills, of writing checks and subtracting numbers, is not at all satisfying, but always impersonal, and always frustrating, because always there is never enough to pay everyone everything. I long then for the pheasants and rabbits on the table, the gun to be cleaned; once or twice a summer I fulfill that need with an afternoon of mackerel fishing with my children.

I know I'm not supposed to yearn for these male pleasures, but I do anyway, and I end with uncertainty; and since these acts of breadwinning have to do with women, it is the women I'm uncertain about. I believe in most of the tenets of the female movement. There are some exceptions; I am bewildered and angered by the iron-clad liberationist whose name escapes me because I never wanted to house it anyway, who said: A man who tries to make a woman have an orgasm is a sexist pig. Which makes me ask: What, then, is a man who doesn't try to make a woman have an orgasm? I am also bothered by the occasional woman who is likely to see any simple gesture as symbolic; once I offered to light a woman's cigarette, but she said: No, I can take care of myself. I had no doubt that she could take care of herself and did not understand why lighting a cigarette had such significance. I was younger then.

Later, though, I became so sympathetic to the sounds of pain from the female soul that I went through androgynous periods when, in a moment of total capitulation, I might have called myself a sexist pig for remembering with nostalgia the dead birds on the kitchen table in Iowa. There were many reasons for this. One was the work of Anton Chekhov, who showed me that a woman's soul has a struggle all its own, neither more nor less serious than a man's, but different. So did John Cheever and Joan Didion and Edna O'Brien, and many others, but Chekhov got there first with the most. There was, though, a deeper force working on me: my own life during five years of bachelorhood, when I listened to many women, women I wasn't involved with, so that I was free to listen to them without concurrently preparing my own defense. I began to feel a special rapport with them, began to see their lives as struggles very close to those of a writer. I am speaking now of women who stay home, and whose children are old enough so that they have left breast, arms, and backpack and, like puppies, are wandering in the lawn smelling new things. Or have finally gone, with new shoes and lunchbox, to that terrible first day of school. These women, like writers, have no time clocks to punch, no waiting boss. I write in the morning before teaching, and neither these women nor I care about the morning commuter traffic. There is no place we have to be. We already are where we have to be, facing ourselves. Both of us, without the prodding of a paycheck or the loss of a job, face only time itself, and our responsibility to use it as best we can. This demands discipline, daily resilience, and a commitment to use time fully, to find or create joy in it, and we must always fear what Hemingway in *A Moveable Feast* calls "the death loneliness that comes at the end of every day that is wasted in your life."

I do not envy those men and women who have jobs instead of true work. But, for some of them, there is this: They know from one minute to the next what they must do at their place of work, they know at the day's end they will feel they have accomplished something, even if it is no more than reporting in at a given hour, staying at a given place, going through motions and speaking words they understand and can even predict, until the hands of the clock reach that algebraic symbol which tells them they can go home. They have put in a day. But the women I'm speaking of can lie on the bathroom floor, staring at the ceiling and courting despair, until the children return loud and hungry at three o'clock. I can leave my desk and stare at the ceiling, too, and no one but I will suffer for it, unless I then turn on those I love, make them pay for my failure. And if the woman rises from the floor at the sound of the children's voices, and passes out the peanut butter sandwiches, vacuums the floor, and girds herself to prepare dinner number three thousand nine hundred and forty-two, feeds the family and is cheerful at dinner, and cleans the kitchen, then she too can lead a life which only she suffers, only she knows is killing her so slowly and relentlessly that by the time it does, she will have long since stopped dreading the end. So, for me, talking to certain women is like talking to a fellow writer.

And why did it take me so long to understand this, and why do I keep losing sight of it, wanting to bring dead birds to a woman whom I want to be happy, even if she has spent the entire day talking to no one but children while mortality screams at her from the walls which are supposed to be her love nest, her home? Because I am fixed in transition, static, pulled one way by my youth, and the other way by what I have learned since then. Very early, I understood that women were required to be other than what they were. When I was thirteen, my sixteen-year-old sister quizzed me on baseball before her dates. I told her the leading teams and hitters, and after one of these catechism lessons, I asked why she had to know about Ted Williams anyway. Because you have to know these things for boys, she said. I asked her what the other girls talked about. They know these things, she said.

The rest of what I learned as a boy gave me that vision of men and women which I had to discard during the first half of this decade, when I was a defrocked husband and was, for the first time since my teenage years, a-courting again, a-hunting again. My parents taught me to open doors for women, pull out chairs for them, to walk on their streetsides so that gutter spray from passing cars would hit me instead of them, to follow them up stairs and precede them down in case they fell, and, in general, to treat them like distant cousins who were making a fragile visit from the mental institutions where they spent their lives. Then there were the household tasks; neither my sisters nor I ever questioned the girls' assignment to kitchen and house-cleaning, and mine to the disposal of garbage and mowing the lawn. It was not until I came, too late, to bachelorhood and shared apartments with men that I learned that food, before it becomes a meal, does not belong strictly to the female province, and that when a meal becomes garbage, it does not belong strictly to the male province. And I further learned that dirty dishes are the responsibility of those who dirty them, as pots and pans are, and floors and rugs and sheets and clothes. My teenage sons are excellent cooks, and my nine-year-old stepson does not suck his thumb in a sudden spasm of sexual disorientation when he sees me pushing a vacuum cleaner, cooking a meal, or washing dishes.

Reading Chekhov helped me into transit; one of his combatants was a character in another book, a harmless enough book for a boy to read, or so it would seem, but it was not harmless, for in my boyhood life of the imagination I learned much from Robin Hood. Not Errol Flynn, the Robin Hood who caused too much emotional swirl, not only in the ladies on the screen but in the audience as well, to make me feel that women should be handled with a delicacy which denied their very souls. No, it was the book that moved me to the sort of angelic devotion to the female, which is finally a form of exclusion, a tyrannical boundary (albeit usually unwitting) between the real world of men and the dream world of women, a world which was of course dreamed by men, not by the women who were held in deleterious yet tender captivity there. I read *Robin Hood* often, and my sisters, both older than I, were pleased by each reading, for in that lingering days-long nimbus of the book, which ends with Robin Hood's murder by a woman, and his dying refusal of Little John's request to kill her, with gentle Robin's saying he had never in his life harmed a woman, and would not have it done in his name after he was dead, I walked about the house like a young boy who has just heard the whispers of angels, and knows that his destiny is sainthood. I brought my sisters and their girl-friends cookies and soft drinks from the kitchen. I deferred, with the humble strength of Robin Hood (no trace of uxori-ousness in that bowman), to all their wishes. I remember riding a city bus with a sister and her friends; we were going to the swimming pool. When I saw that I had taken a seat too soon, that one of those eleven- or twelve-year-old girls was left standing, I quickly rose and gave her my seat and stood holding the hand bar, pretending not to hear my sister murmur to her friend: He's been reading *Robin Hood* again. On her face was a sweet smile of victory, the sort of victory women got in those days.

So I remain static, pulled backward by my early years (they probably add up to thirty or more) and by Robin

Hood, the hunter whose bow provided meat, the merry drinker of ale whose adventures and games and joy were with men, and whose purity and tender strength were given to women. And I am pulled forward by what I know, and I try to learn to erase the old boundaries, to see women as they are and I suppose always were: creatures like me, who live in the same world I live in, who do not need me to keep them from being splashed by cars, from falling down stairs. But boyhood is hard to leave, and perhaps one never does, and while I try to become a man of the times, I ask you, O ladies, for neither absolution nor understanding. All I ask is a smile. That wise and affectionate smile that only a woman can give.

1977

The Judge and Other Snakes

I will call the girl Jan. She was fifteen on that autumn
night, early autumn, a warm Sunday night, the baseball
season not yet ended. The young male who attacked her I
will call Nick; he was twenty-one. Jan was sixteen by the
morning of the trial in December. At the trial, The Judge
referred to Jan and Nick as Eve and Adam: "What we have
here is a typical case of Adam and Eve and the snake in the
garden."

I suppose The Judge was trying to be colorful, to sound
experienced and wise; but to me he seemed bored, impa-
tient, and finally angry. He was also inaccurate. Jan was not
seduced into tasting the fruit of the tree of knowledge; nor
did she persuade Nick to share her sin. She did not cause
The Fall, and the condemnation to mortality and the sweat
of the brow. And she and Nick were not banished together,
to enter the world, to mate, and have children. She did,
though, pour what she called punch onto Nick's car and its

upholstery. One cup of it, with perhaps a swallow or two gone, purchased at the Midway Pizza and Subs on South Main Street in Bradford, which is part of the city of Haverhill, Massachusetts.

There were, though, some snakes: six or eight or more punks, males in their late teens or early twenties. I can call them neither boys nor men. It is possible that I recall my boyhood with a nostalgia that distorts, that too partially compares those years in the early nineteen fifties with what I see now. But I do not believe this. I would vividly remember seeing a boy shoving or striking or choking a girl. Certainly in the adult world, behind windows and walls, men were beating women. But not where we could see them, even when we were sixteen and drank in the two night clubs that, in Lafayette, Louisiana, would serve us liquor; and the other clubs in nearby towns, where we drank and played the jukebox, sometimes with dates, sometimes without: four or five of us boys at a table, drinking gin bucks or Seven and Sevens or bourbon and Cokes or Falstaffs, and smoking Lucky Strikes or Philip Morris from brown packages, and wearing ducktails and suede shoes. Not even in those clubs where older couples drank and danced, college students and working people: cheerful and feisty Cajuns and Creoles, with accents whose source was eighteenth- and nineteenth-century French, and a few drawling southerners, most of them Protestants. Not even there, in the dark and the music, among couples who were lovers or married, and so on the dance floor and at the tables there were elements of violence: passion and heartbreak as tangible as the sweat soaking through their shirts and blouses, and dripping on their brows, their cheeks.

But we never saw a man hit a woman; and if we had, I know that the other men and boys would not have watched.

They would have left their girls and women at the tables and on the dance floor and swarmed on the woman-hitter before the bouncer or bartender could reach him. In the Marine Corps I knew a staff sergeant who told me of sitting one night at a bar in San Francisco. A couple beside him were quarreling. Then the man slapped the woman, knocking her off the stool onto the floor. The sergeant got up and punched the man and knocked him to the floor. The man and woman then turned on the sergeant, the woman using a beer bottle on his head, and during his beating the sergeant realized they were husband and wife, and so vowed never again to interfere with marriages, save on an adulterous bed. But that was in the late fifties or early sixties, and my high school and college years in bars were in the fifties, and everything has changed now, and no one seems to know why, and I don't know why, and to blame it on female liberation is I believe not too simple, but too shallow.

I spent much of my boyhood as a moving target for bullies, both the perennials who bloomed each fall and lived in the classroom and at recess through the school year, then in May were gone; and the occasional bullies of summer: boys on a baseball diamond or at the public swimming pool or at the golf course or dances at the community center. When I got my driver's license at sixteen, I weighed 105 pounds. The following summer, construction work and beer-drinking gave me twenty more. Then I was a high school senior. Then I was an eighteen-year-old, 125-pound college freshman, destined by my body and my feelings about it to enter a Marine officer candidate program. I record these pounds because for a long time, much too long, I believed they alone were the scents that drew a bully as garbage in the sea draws sharks. My two sons were both small boys, and they drew bullies too, until the oldest, while still in high school, built himself a new body with barbells and dumbells, and the youngest simply grew broad and tall and strong. The bullying did not stop, though, until each of them had stood his ground and fought and won and learned that inside his body each had a spirit which demanded respect from itself, and would prefer injury to cowardice. My sons are grown men now, and we often talk about bullies, and what they did to us, and why they did it.

Our size was not the scent that drew them. It was our faces, and our movements in the world: as much as we tried to walk, and sit, and talk with confidence, we were transparent. And if our motions and voices did not betray us, our lips and eyes did: they showed the discerning eye of bullies what a wiser person, perhaps an older girl, may have recognized as the roots of vanity. What the bullies saw in our faces was fear; not fear of physical injury, as we believed then, but of humiliation, not only from the fists of a bully, but in all the forms it took in our boyhoods: public mistakes in the classroom or athletic field; not on written examinations, but mistakes our classmates could see. The bullies chose us over other boys who were as small, because a bully's distorted focus is, like any pervert's, out of proportion. The bully saw in us not the whole boy our friends saw, but that fulfillment of his need: boys who would bear anything from him with no resistance at all, save hiding or running away.

My sons and I realize now that bullies never fought. In a classroom of boys from the first through the twelfth grades, there are usually some fighters. They are not bullies. They are easily provoked and at once become motion, action. The ones I knew were good company, most of them athletes, and I respected them and warmly drew safety from being with them. They walked on a different earth than the bullies did: we were in the same classrooms, and on the same playgrounds at recess and at athletic hour, but the fighters and bullies moved about, oblivious of each other, like wild animals at an African watering hole when the predators are not hungry.

When the fighters were nearby we were safe, for the bullies retreated into their strange — and estranged — dark selves. Once, when I was a boy, some of us promoted a fight between our bully and one of the classroom fighters, who also fought in the boxing ring. I do not recall how we did this, but since we were cowards we probably used lies, whispered into the fighter's ear that the bully had said this, and that, and so forth. After school we gathered behind a canebrake: three or four Iagos and the two boys we used, and I imagine my comrades in cowardice felt the same cool shiver of self-hatred that I did, the same glimmer of recognition: that now we were the bullies, hoping for catharsis through the body and — we did not know it — the spirit of our boxer. The bully did not fight. He took the pre-fight abuse that boys use to increase their adrenaline until they can throw a punch, indeed cannot do anything but throw a punch: the bully took shoves and insults, and retreated and denied the reason for a fight, and so denied us. He was a dark-skinned Cajun boy, and in the new pallor of his face I saw my own fears. And still was too young to know the meaning of that pale and frightened face.

Our fighter was bigger than the bully, and I thought again it was all a matter of size, and hated my lack of it, and walked home from school with that self-pity steeped in remorse that rose from a sin I could not name. The bully was, in fact, as small as I was; our only differences were his muscles, and my soft arms and cowardice. And the cowardice was not, as I believed, physical: it was broader and deeper than that, and touched nearly all my public actions. Its source was a frightened absorption with myself that spawned pride and vanity as often as cowardice: the A's in school, the fluent and falsely humble answers in the classroom, the virtuous and solemn face returning from the Communion rail to the pew, where I knelt and bowed my head and closed my eyes and, as the Host dissolved on my tongue, I prayed with the fervor of the painted profile of Christ kneeling before a large stone in the Garden of Olives, asking that His cup be lifted. Kneeled and prayed that way for anyone to see, and I believed that everyone but those kneeling in front of me saw, and that was the source of my vanity and my cowardice: always I believed everyone was watching me.

I have outgrown that, and I believe my sons have too. We talk of a man we know who one morning shaved the beard he had worn for years and went downstairs for breakfast with the family and no one noticed; and of a woman I know, who for over twenty years was the only cigarette smoker in her family, and her husband and several children wanted her to stop, and teased her, begged her, scolded her; finally she did stop, and neither her husband nor her children were aware of this, and at dinner after her first week without a cigarette she finally told them. And my sons and I are able now to laugh, to say: No wonder those bullies beat us up; they *should* have. We know now that if we had fought the first bully who harassed us, we would have saved ourselves years of torment.

Because of all this, and I hope a sense of justice as well, I become enraged whenever I see the strong bullying the weak. And when the weak one is a female, my rage is deeper. Because with girls and women, it is all a matter of size. Few women, no matter how courageous, can defeat a man in physical combat, if both she and he are normally made. So what was — or still is — in the hearts of those snakes who watched while Adam beat Eve, Nick pushed and struck and choked young Jan?

I understand them less than I understand Nick, and I understand very little about him, or about the young woman who was with him that night, his girlfriend who not only continued to be his girlfriend after his assault on Jan, but was in the courtroom in December, waiting to take the stand and commit perjury. But I can recognize Nick's rage, and his girlfriend's loyalty. The unrecognizable emotion, for me, is whatever stirred and churned inside the ones who watched. It was not fear that held them; they were Nick's friends.

Because these punks abound, I have in the trunk of the car an axe handle. Two autumns earlier, in 1982, also at the Midway Pizza and Sub, some of these snakes beat up students from the college where I used to work. The students were foreigners, and I believe there were three of them. The beating was on a Saturday night, and I heard about it the next afternoon, and Sunday night I lay awake until eight o'clock in the morning. The anger and pain that turned my bed into a cage, and changed the silence of night into the imagined sounds of fists and feet striking flesh and bone, had nothing to do with townies and students. I had no such loyalties; I often told students that my children were townies, and so was I. Nor was I disturbed because the students were foreign; if they had been Samoans — I suppose there are small ones but I have never seen one — or Japanese sumo wrestlers, or if they had been well-built young men from any nation; or, lacking the physiques, if they had possessed that certain earned or sometimes feigned aura that deters bullies, they would have simply gone into the place and bought their food and returned to the campus. These Middle Eastern students on that warm Saturday night were small; the bullies assaulted in a pack and beat them at will, beat them until none of the students could rise from the sidewalk.

I did not spend all of that long Sunday night imagining the beating. The Midway is on the main street of Haverhill, and is between the bar where a poet and I used to go for nightcaps, and the street where we lived. So during much of that night I thought of Mike and myself driving home after our beers and seeing the punks again, with victims or a victim. What would we do, since we had no choice but to get out of the car and force a gang to cease and desist?

Because of horrors inflicted on too many women I love, I carry a licensed handgun when I go with a woman to Boston. Lately, because one is liable now in America to turn a street corner and walk into lethal violence whose target is of either gender, and of any age — a small child, an old woman or man — I have begun to carry a gun whenever I go to Boston. As much as I have thought about it, I still believe I do not carry it for myself, would not even use it to protect myself, except from death. This is not bravery; I simply don't care if someone takes my money, and don't particularly care if someone decides to pound me about the head and shoulders. In either case, I would not resort to a gun. There is nothing wrong with taking flight, if you are the only target. On that insomniac night in the fall of 1982 I decided I would not carry a gun to my neighborhood bar; that if I felt a need to do that, it was time to move to Canada.

So I considered weapons. I wanted one I could keep in the trunk of the Subaru, one that I would use only to prevent or try to stop local violence. I suppose I believe that nearly always we are unprepared: we have forgotten first-aid training, we don't know where the phone is, we are alone and weaponless and have no skills in what are strangely called the martial arts, or in boxing (an under-rated skill: in a bar when I was in high school I saw a state champion high-school boxer back down four punks whose belligerence turned to obsequiousness when they heard his name; they knew his speed and power, knew their numbers only meant that he would knock four of them to the floor, rather than just one); so I also believe that many — not enough, but many — newspaper stories we read about people doing nothing while another human being is in trouble are stories not about apathy but about not knowing what to do, and the stasis of fear that accompanies that condition. I suppose I believe, too, that if you are prepared, you will not suddenly be in the midst of trouble. If you know what to do when someone has an epileptic seizure (I learned one afternoon in Haverhill, frightening on-the-job training that left me in near shock), and have in your purse or pocket a tongue depressor, then someone will suffer a seizure out of your field of vision, standing some three blocks away in a movie line. If this means I believe in luck, then it follows that I believe in bad luck more than good. The optimism in this is the belief that if you are prepared, you will not be called upon, and can go about your life in peace.

I quickly discarded the idea of a knife. I carry one any-way, as I have in my pocket since boyhood, and for the same reason: every boy had a knife. I also carry it for the few times when I need to open a package, or slice cheese or apples outside of a house. In Marine officer candidate train-ing, a very quick and graceful sergeant taught us to fight with knives, and to fight unarmed against one. But only after the admonishment: *If anyone ever pulls a knife on you,*

67

run. Besides, drawing a knife on a pack of punks is a weak defensive measure; it is only effective if you use it very quickly and seriously and therefore dangerously: you must attack human flesh with a blade. I only wanted a defensive weapon. I discarded, too, the next object that came to mind: a baseball bat. That heavy end could cause a concussion, fracture a skull. Then I remembered the pugil stick: a round wooden pole with large cylindrical pads on both ends. We used it in the Marines to practice bayonet fighting; we wore football helmets, and learned to use the rifle and bayonet as a boxer uses his fists: jabs, crosses, uppercuts, hooks, the butt of the rifle serving as one fighting end, the bayonet as the other. So an axe handle: light wood that I could grasp at its middle, using either end on noses, mouths, jaws, and so forth, and with little danger of inflicting serious injury but with the probability of slowing down and finally taking the fight out of these bullies who do not like to fight anyway. Once I decided on the weapon I knew I would never have to use it. That Monday afternoon I bought it at a local hardware store and when the young man rang up the sale he said: "That reminds me of a movie. I can't remember which one."

"Walking Tall," I said, and put it in the trunk where for two years it stayed, losing its brightness, moistening, drying, collecting dust. I forgot it was there, save when I stacked suitcases on it, or shoved it aside to make room for an ice chest.

I remembered it at once on that Sunday night nearly two years later. I was alone at the bar, talking to the bartender and some regulars, and I left at eleven o'clock to watch the baseball news at eleven-fifteen. In Yankee Stadium that afternoon the Red Sox had won, Boyd had pitched, Rice had homered, and I wanted to see the highlights. I was still in second gear when I saw them: a crowd on the right side of the street, beyond the sidewalk; they were in a semi-circle, watching something at the drugstore wall. I turned the car toward them, drove it to the curb, and brightened the headlights. Some of the punks turned to the light. Past their faces I saw what they were watching: a tall young punk holding a sobbing and screaming girl; he was pushing her back and head against a brick wall, pulling her forward, pushing her again and again. I wanted my sons: my two big justice-seeking sons. I got out of the car, leaving the lights on, went back to the trunk, picked up the axe handle, re-turned to the front of the car and stood in the lights. Some of the punks shouted at me to go mind my own fucking business. That line strikes me still: my business, while Jan's back and head were striking a brick wall. I told them I wanted the girl left alone. There was more shouting, and Nick let go of Jan, who fled down the street. He ran after her, caught her by the post office, and I heard her sobbing and yelling. Then Nick came toward me. He stood close and yelled at me and I asked him why a man his size was hitting a woman. With a querulous nuance in his rage, he shouted that she had thrown a drink on his car, even on the seat. Then I saw the cruiser stopping across the street and an officer coming out of the passenger side and walking toward us and I told Nick a police officer was coming up behind him. The officer dispersed the punks and listened to Nick and me telling our stories, while the driver of the cruiser drove diagonally across the street, into the opposite lane, his blue lights flashing, and stopped beside us. I leaned into his window. Beyond him, in the passenger seat, was Jan. She was weeping into the palms of her hands. I gave the officer my name, address, phone number, and told Jan I would be a witness in court, then drove home and saw

Boyd pitching and Rice hitting a home run.

Jan or her mother or sometimes both of them, passing the phone between them, called me during the next few weeks, to let me know what they were doing about the assault and battery charges against Nick, and the date of the pre-trial hearing before the magistrate. They did not have a telephone in their home. They had a very old car. Jan was fifteen; by the date of the trial in December she was sixteen and had left high school and enrolled in a school for beauticians. An older brother lived at home with them. The father lived in Lawrence, some fifteen or twenty minutes away, but was no longer a father; neither Jan nor her mother ever mentioned him and he was not at the trial, where I learned of his existence on earth from Jan's maternal grandmother.

On the Sunday night of her beating Jan had walked from her home to Bradford Square: two blocks of shops for pizza, hamburgers, roast beef, and the bar where I was a regular. She was to meet Nick at the Midway Pizza and Sub. But when she walked into that small brightly lit place where teenagers ate pizza and drank soft drinks and smoked cigarettes, Nick was with another girl; perhaps she was a young woman. At the trial she looked nineteen or twenty, but she was dressed, made-up, and bejeweled as for a Saturday night date, so I could not guess her age. Jan believed Nick was her boyfriend. When she saw him in the booth with the blonde instead of a space beside him for her, she went to the counter and bought a paper cup of punch, whatever that may be; then she asked Nick to come outside. They quarreled; they had a date but he was with someone else. Then she tossed her punch onto his car and some went through the window, where gravity pulled it to his upholstery. His car was new, devoutly cared for, American. He attacked her: pushing, hitting, and once he held her over a park bench: pressing her back down across the back of the bench, he choked her with both of his hands. He is a tall creature and his hands are not small and I imagine they were very strong as they squeezed Jan's throat.

That night the two officers in the cruiser drove Jan to her home, only a few blocks away; her mother took her to Hale Hospital in Haverhill, where they treated and recorded her bruises and abrasions. On Monday Jan's mother drove her to the Essex County Court House in Haverhill, and Jan pressed charges. Her mother told me on one of the calls from a pay phone that she had discovered, after Nick beat Jan, that he was twenty-one years old; she said if she had known this she would not have allowed Jan to see him.

The magistrate's hearing was in a small office at the court house, and while we waited I met Jan's mother and, for the first time, saw Jan: not from a distance, screaming and crying, as Nick pushed her against bricks, and not weeping into her hands in the light of the cruiser. That morning she was anxious, neatly dressed, and lovely, with long soft blonde hair. I offered her a cigarette and we smoked and waited until a tall stocky officer in plain clothes called us into the small room. The magistrate, holding an unlit but recently smoked cigar, sat behind a table; Nick sat beside him: tall and handsome, and conscious of his looks. Swagger was in his face, his perfectly combed-back dark hair, his smooth shave. His dark eyes were interesting: they were not wary or attentive or humble; they were intense and angry, the eyes of a man unjustly treated. Jan sat opposite the magistrate, her mother opposite Nick, and I stood behind Jan and the officer stood behind Nick. The magistrate asked Jan if I were a relative or close friend; she said she had never seen me until that Sunday night. This is why I was her only witness, on the advice of the young lawyer from the district attorney's office: her other witnesses were friends, two girls, the only people who had tried to stop Nick. All males at the Midway Pizza and Sub were Nick's friends. The magistrate asked Jan for her story; she was nervous, but she had good control, and told the story calmly, chronologically, until she reached the moment when Nick attacked her. He loudly interrupted, said she was lying, and the magistrate turned to him and said: "Shut up. You'll get your turn."

Then he asked Jan to go on with her story and when she finished, Nick started, his voice rising: it was all a lie, he had done nothing, he — The magistrate said: "Did you touch her?"

Nick lowered his voice: "I touched her jacket."

The magistrate slapped the table, said: "Assault and battery; tell it to the judge," and dismissed us.

On a Friday morning in December my wife and I went to the trial. My wife sat in the rear and I sat beside Jan and her mother and grandmother. I had forgotten to borrow a necktie but I wore a jacket and my one pair of winter slacks and my wife had trimmed my hair. *Make friends with the children of Mammon.* As a man said to me once: *There are seven Boston women dead because they believed in the American idea of respectability: they let the Boston Strangler into their homes; he always dressed well.* Nick sat at a table with his lawyer, near the judge's bench, and he wore a dark three-piece suit. His girlfriend, his only witness, sat to our right, across the aisle from our benches. During the other cases we watched, I whispered to Jan, again and again, that she need not worry. She was afraid of speaking from the stand, she was afraid Nick would be found not guilty ("I'm afraid we'll lose," she said), and her mother was angry because the assistant district attorney did not have and had never seen the hospital records showing what Nick had done to Jan back in the warmth of the baseball season's final days. That young lawyer had also waited until less than an hour before we entered the court room to ask me what I had seen Nick do to Jan.

She took the stand first, stood with a good posture, a raised face looking directly at the clerk as she swore to tell the truth, with that anachronistic oath, the truth itself an anachronism in the land, something to be searched for by archaeologists of the human heart, the saints Dorothy Day said again and again we must have in this country. Then The Judge did something strange: he explained to Jan the Fifth Amendment. Then he said there were counter charges arising in the case. I left my seat and crossed the aisle and sat at the rail, behind a young lawyer, a friend of mine; he was on the other side of the flimsy spoked wall, the side reserved for justice. I asked him what The Judge was doing.

"I think he's going to throw out the case," he said.

"Throw it out?"

"That's why he's warning her about what to admit on the stand."

"Oh my God."

And The Judge was indeed warning Jan about charges of malicious damage of property and assault with a knife. As she watched him and listened, her face flushed: in confusion, and probably in the knowledge that all morning she had been right, as we waited through the other cases; that during the months since her beating she had been right: she would not win. She would lose because she was bound to, as she was bound to be hurt when a twenty-one-year-old male attacked her. Oh, but she was good. I doubt that she will ever recall how good she was, because the morning was so horrible for her. I hope she can. The assistant district attorney asked: "What were you doing while the defendant held you over the back of the park bench and strangled you?"

Standing up there, she looked down at his face and said: "I was trying to breathe."

We have not made a country where there is a lot of room for Jan and people like her to breathe. I believe The Judge threw out the case because Jan was a girl (and now, God willing, a woman, alive on the earth, with that morning in court and the night of her beating and the time between them still part of her); and because the judge is old, and tired of people and their continual pain before his bench, and because Jan is not, as the phrase goes, from a prominent family. I will never believe that if her family were wealthy he would have done to her what he did. For Nick was and is a punk, and the large officer at the magistrate's hearing said to me after the magistrate sent the case to court: *Now we've got him.*

I did not get to the stand. The Judge stopped Jan and the prosecuting attorney and sent Jan back to her seat, with her mother and grandmother. I still sat across the aisle from them, behind my lawyer friend, asking him what was happening now, what the fuck was happening *now*? Because The Judge called the defense and the prosecution to the bench and spoke to them, and my friend said: "It's all over, he's throwing it out."

The two lawyers went back to their tables and The Judge said: "I'm going to dismiss this case. What we have here is a classic case of Adam and Eve and the Snake in the Garden. You, young man," he said, his voice low, "the next time you're with a girl, you keep your hands to yourself. Do you understand me?"

Nick told his honor that he did. Then the judge looked at Jan beyond the railing, among the spectators, and those awaiting trial. He spoke loudly, with anger: "And as for you, young lady — Stand up."

She stood erectly while her face reddened and tears flowed down her cheeks and she remained silent as his voice rose.

"You are the prime instigator in this case. You started it all, and I strongly advise you in the future to control your temper; that's all."

I watched her standing, her back and shoulders still straight, and I watched her face. Then I raised my hand and stood and softly his honor acknowledged me, and softly I asked to address the court, and politely he said Yes. Not so softly then I said that I could not believe that here in this court in the United States of America in the nineteen eighties I had just heard what I had heard. I said: Your honor, I was *there;* I saw him banging her head against a brick wall; he could have killed her.

His honor was talking too, but I did not hear him. My lawyer friend shook my hand, and I left the court room, to gather in the adjoining room with my wife, the prosecuting attorney, Jan's mother and grandmother, to join in voiced anger and disbelief as Nick and his girlfriend walked past us, arm-in-arm: the girl who was going to take the stand and testify that Jan had attacked Nick with a knife. Either the prosecutor did not know about this until The Judge called him and Nick's lawyer to the bench, or he chose not to talk about it with Jan, or with anyone else, until we stood together. There was a knife: a penknife that had belonged to

Jan's grandmother; it fell from her purse when Nick held her down, her back on top of the park bench's back, as he choked her. Then I looked around for Jan. She sat on a bench against a wall, crying, and I went over and held her and sobbing she said: "I got beat up. He beat me up, and nothing *hap*pened."

We all left the court house. It was noon and cold and the sun was low, at its winter angle, beyond the city and the Merrimack River. In the car I said to my wife: "She did everything she was supposed to. How will she ever believe in the system again? *Why* should she?"

Then we drove home and I went to bed and slept and woke to the early dark of winter.

1985/1986

On Charon's Wharf

Since we are all terminally ill, each breath and step and day one closer to the last, I must consider those sacraments which soothe our passage. I write on a Wednesday morning in December when snow covers the earth, the sky is grey, and only the evergreens seem alive. This morning I received the sacrament I still believe in: at seven-fifteen the priest elevated the host, then the chalice, and spoke the words of the ritual, and the bread became flesh, the wine became blood, and minutes later I placed on my tongue the taste of forgiveness and of love that affirmed, perhaps celebrated, my being alive, my being mortal. This has nothing to do with immortality, with eternity; I love the earth too much to contemplate a life apart from it, although I believe in that life. No, this has to do with mortality and the touch of flesh, and my belief in the sacrament of the Eucharist is simple: without touch, God is a monologue, an idea, a philosophy; he must touch and be touched, the tongue on flesh, and that touch is the result of the monologues, the idea, the philosophies which led to faith; but in the instant of the touch there is no place for thinking, for talking; the silent touch affirms all that, and goes deeper: it affirms the mysteries of love and mortality.

And that is why I am drawn again and again to see Bergman's *The Seventh Seal,* to watch the knight who, because finally he has been told by Death that he is going to die, must now act within that knowledge, and for the rest of the movie he lives in constant touch with his mortality, as we all should every day, with everyone (but we don't, we don't, we are distracted, we run errands ...); and that is why one of my favorite scenes in the movie is the knight sitting on the earth with the young couple and their child, and the woman offers him a bowl of berries: he reaches out with both hands, receives the bowl from her, and eats; and the scene is invested with his awareness that his time is confused and lonely and fearful and short, but for these moments, with these people, with this gift of food, he has been given an eternal touch: eternal because, although death will destroy him, it cannot obliterate the act between him and the woman. She has given him the food. He has taken it. In the face of time, the act is completed. Death cannot touch it now, can only finally stop the hearts that were united in it.

So many of us fail: we divorce wives and husbands, we leave the roofs of our lovers, go once again into the lonely march, mustering our courage with work, friends, half-pleasures which are not whole because they are not shared. Yet still I believe in love's possibility, in its presence on the earth; as I believe I can approach the altar on any morning of any day which may be the last and receive the touch that does not, for me, say: There is no death; but does say: In this instant I recognize, with you, that you must die. And I believe I can do this in an ordinary kitchen with an ordinary woman and five eggs. The woman sets the table. She watches me beat the eggs. I scramble them in a saucepan, as my now-dead friend taught me; they stand deeper and cook softer, he said. I take our plates, spoon eggs on them, we sit and eat. She and I and the kitchen have become extraordinary: we are not simply eating; we are pausing in the march to perform an act together; we are in love; and the meal offered and received is a sacrament which says: I know you will die; I am sharing food with you; it is all I can do, and it is everything.

As lovers we must have these sacraments, these actions which restore our focus, and therefore ourselves. For our lives are hurried and much too distracted, and one of the strangest and most dangerous of all distractions is this lethargy of self we suffer from, this part of ourselves that does not want to get out of bed and once out of bed does not want to dress and once dressed does not want to prepare breakfast and once fed does not want to work. And what does it want? Perhaps it wants nothing at all. It is a mystery, a lovely one because it is human, but it is also dangerous. Some days it does not want to love, and we yield to it, we drop into an abyss whose walls echo with strange dialogues. These dialogues are with the beloved, and at their center is a repetition of the word *I* and sometimes *you*, but neither word now is uttered with a nimbus of blessing. These are the nights when we sit in that kitchen and talk too long and too much, so that the words multiply each other, and what they express — pain, doubt, anxiousness, dread — becomes emotions which are not rooted in our true (or better) selves, which exist apart from those two gentle people who shared eggs at this same table which now is soiled with ashes and glass-rings.

These nights can destroy us. With words we create genies which rise on the table between us, and fearfully we watch them hurt each other; they look like us, they sound like us, but they are not us, and we want to call them back, see them disappear like shriveling clouds back into our throats, down into our hearts where they can join our other selves and be forced again into their true size: a small *I* among many other *I*'s. We try this with more words and too often the words are the wrong ones, the genies grow, and we are approaching those hours after midnight when lovers should never quarrel, for the night has its mystery too and will not be denied, it loves to distort the way we feel and if we let it, it will. We say: But wait a minute ... But you said ... But I always thought that ... Well how do you think I feel, who do you think you are anyway? Just who in the hell do you think you *are*?

There are no answers, at least not at that table. Each day she is several women, and I am several men. We must try to know each other, understand each other, and love each other as best as we can. But we cannot know and understand all of each other. This is a time in our land when lovers talk to each other, and talk to counselors about each other, and talk to counselors in front of each other. We have to do this. Many of us grew up in homes whose table and living room conversations could have been recorded in the daily newspaper without embarrassing anyone, and now we want very much to explore each other, and to be explored. We are like children in peril, though, when we believe this exploring can be done with words alone, and that the exploring must always give answers, and that the exploring is love itself rather than a way to deepen it. For then we kill our hearts with talk, we place knowing and understanding higher than love, and failing at the first two, as we sometimes must, we believe we have failed at the third. Perhaps we have not. But when you believe you no longer love, you no longer do.

I need and want to give the intimacy we achieve with words. But words are complex: at times too powerful or fragile or simply wrong; and they are affected by a tone of voice, a gesture of a hand, a light in the eyes. And words are sometimes autonomous little demons who like to form their own parade and march away, leaving us behind. Once in a good counselor's office I realized I was not telling the truth. It was not that I meant to lie. She was asking me questions and I was trying to answer them, and I was indeed answering them. But I left out *maybe, perhaps, I wonder....* Within minutes I was telling her about emotions I had not felt. But by then I was feeling what I was telling her, and that is the explosive nitroglycerin seeping through the hearts of lovers.

So what I want and want to give, more than the intimacy of words, is shared ritual, the sacraments. I believe that, without those, all our talking, no matter how enlightened, will finally drain us, divide us into two confused and frustrated people, then destroy us as lovers. We are of the flesh, and we must turn with faith toward that truth. We need the companion on the march, the arms and lips and body against the dark of the night. It is our flesh which lives in time and will die, and it is our love which comforts the flesh. Beneath all the words we must have this daily acknowledgment from the beloved, and we must give it too or pay the lonely price of not living fully in the world: that as lovers we live on Charon's wharf, and he's out there somewhere in that boat of his, and today he may row in to where we sit laughing, and reach out to grasp an ankle, hers or mine.

It would be madness to try to live so intensely as lovers that every word and every gesture between us was a sacrament, a pure sign that our love exists despite and perhaps even because of our mortality. But we can do what the priest does, with his morning consecration before entering the routine of his day; what the communicant does in that instant of touch, that quick song of the flesh, before he goes to work. We can bring our human, distracted love into focus with an act that doesn't need words, an act which dramatizes for us what we are together. The act itself can be anything: five beaten and scrambled eggs, two glasses of wine, running beside each other in rhythm with the pace and breath of the beloved. They are all parts of that loveliest of all sacraments between man and woman, that passionate harmony of flesh whose breath and dance and murmur says: We are, we are, we *are* . . .

1977

Part Three

∋•⟨

After Twenty Years

I PROMISED TO write a reminiscence about my two and a half years as a student at the Iowa Writer's Workshop, but this morning I read the mail before going to my desk and, after reading a letter from my twenty-six-year-old son, I could no longer write about my life in a good place from mid-January 1964 until mid-August 1966. I was going to write that I learned much at Iowa, more even than I knew I was learning then, and always I was learning. I was deeply grateful to my teachers and to my faculty friends who were not my teachers in classrooms but taught me anyway. When I left Iowa and began teaching more than a graduate assistant's load, my gratitude became awe. I truly did not understand how those men had given so much of themselves in the classroom, in conferences, and in bars and their homes and our homes and on the phone.

Here's what my son, Andre III, wrote from New York City:

I saw two men sleeping on a grate in front of the Waldorf-Astoria last Friday night. It was around midnight and I was just walking around. . . . One of the men was black, the other white. Both were clean shaven. Both were in work clothes and long Salvation-Army-looking overcoats. Both had shoes. Both looked and smelled sober while they slept. They had their duffle bags in their laps. *And I'm convinced they did not know each other.* They looked like two strangers sharing some warmth. Women in fur coats and men in five hundred dollar suits and coats did not even pause in their banter as they passed them on their way to a stretch limousine and dinner. Did you read about Evelio Javier today, the Harvard-educated Marcos foe and provincial leader of Aquino's campaign, who was chased across a town square in that country by six masked gunmen then slaughtered in an outhouse in somebody's backyard? He was forty-two. It happened in San José de Buenavista. What did Anne Frank write in her diary? "In spite of everything, I still believe people are really good at heart."

Peace, Pop.

These days I barely have the heart, the will, to do something as insignificant as writing fiction. I cannot write about something as trifling as my life at Iowa, where my first wife and I thought we were poor because we had four children and a twenty-four-hundred-dollar a year assistantship and surplus food every month and I sold blood for twenty-five dollars a pint every three months and earned a hundred dollars a month teaching the Britannica Schools Correspondence Course; in my final year Richard Braddock and Paul Engle gave me a thirty-six-hundred-dollar assistantship, and we were no longer eligible for surplus food. Our children never knew we were poor. And of course we weren't. As Joe Williams said during his performance at a jazz club near here, about nine years ago: *There's poor, and there's po'.*

I have always known that writing fiction had little effect on the world; that if it did, young men would not have gone to war after *The Iliad*. Only the privileged — those with homes and food and the luxury of time in a home — are touched, moved, sometimes changed by literature. For the twenty million Americans who are hungry tonight, for the homeless freezing tonight, literature is as useless as a knowledge of astronomy. What do stars look like on a clear cold winter night, when your children are hungry, are daily losing their very health; or when, alone, you look up from a heat grate? Of course in cities at night you can't even see the stars.

C. J. Koch's *The Year of Living Dangerously* is not only one of the best novels I've read in decades but the only one I recall that confronts mass poverty and the callousness of the powerful, the wealthy, and the futility of those who do not despise the poor, who even love them, grieve for them, and can do nothing. Yet still it is a novel, of no use to the poor unless they can eat it, drink it, wear it, use it as a home, and still that is not enough. I believe Koch would agree. There is much pain in his book. Perhaps that is one of the reasons he now lives in Tasmania.

My new young wife and three-and-a-half-year-old daughter and I are living now on nine hundred dollars a month, because I tried to follow the example of my Iowa teachers, and after eighteen years, exhaustion and high blood pressure drove me to retirement, to normal blood pressure and serenity; and still we are not poor. Tonight I watched a movie on the VCR. Even as I write this I am listening to Donizetti's *Lucia di Lammermoor* with Joan Sutherland and Pavarotti, on a Panasonic stereo cassette player, and I am wearing ear phones so I will not wake my sleeping family. I am not hungry. My wife and daughter are not hungry.

We are warm. Outside ice covers the bare branches of trees, and earlier they shone in the light from our one neighbor's house; so did the ice-covered snow under the trees, and between our houses. I stepped outside and looked for a while at that shining white beauty in the peaceful quiet here on the hill in the country. Then I stepped back into the warmth of the kitchen and now, hours later, I remember R. V. Cassill saying: *Nature isn't lethal; it's indifferent.* And I sit with a pen and a notebook and Sutherland and Pavarotti while across the land cold air and frozen snow are lethal: for my indifferent country has made them so: made them silent air raids on our people.

We were not poor at Iowa City, my brave young wife Pat, and me, and our children: Suzanne, born in 1958; Andre in 1959, Jeb in 1960, Nicole in 1963. We had all the time we wanted to spend with each other and with our new and good friends. We had time to read, to talk, even to think. We had time, my wife and I, to make love and a place where we could read about and talk about our Church's opinions and pronouncements about artificial birth control; and to decide that we could resort to contraception and still receive the Catholic sacraments. We had time to love each other, to understand better the complexity of marital love, and to try to achieve what we understood. So we had time to fail; and our later failure, nearly four years after leaving Iowa City,

88

probably began there. But we suffered no more than our friends whose marriages ended. We will never know what our children suffered, and can only hope they are healed now; or will be: if there is complete healing, so long as memory exists.

Our children did not know we had very little money, and they did not know their parents would fail. Nor did we. One day there was an ice storm and when it was over the six of us looked out the living room window at the sparkling trees. We were all very young then, and had lived only on Marine and Navy bases and in small towns, and none of us knew that such beauty was, in the wrong nation, a killer of human beings. I see us now at that window: the red-haired little girl, the two blond boys, the blond girl and the blond mother and me, and I know that the only poverty afflicting my wife and me in Iowa City was youth: educated, Caucasian, never affluent but always safe youth. We knew about blacks, and because we had lived and had two sons at Camp Pendleton, California, we knew about migrant Mexican workers. But at the window we believed in the promise of these moments with our children, and believed that all white Americans could feel as we did, our six bodies pressed together as we exclaimed and pointed and murmured, and looked through cold glass at that afternoon's lovely gift from the sky.

1986

INTO THE SILENCE

FROM TIME TO time I've read or heard a strange notion: many writers come from the South, because southerners have a tradition of telling stories. I did not grow up in the true South. I grew up in southern Louisiana, in a place of Cajuns and Creoles and Catholics. In the neighborhood where I spent most of my boyhood, only a few girls and boys were Protestants. Most of us came home on Ash Wednesday with dark grey crosses on our foreheads. From the third through the twelfth grades I learned from Christian Brothers at Cathedral School in Lafayette. The first class of the day was religion, and the Brothers told stories: from the Old and New Testaments and the lives of the saints, and they also told stories to show and dramatize morality. And through the rest of the day, in other classes, they told us stories, in their worthy attempt to teach us about the earth and its people, the living and the dead. They were not southerners. Two were from France; and Pancho

Villa had sent one out of Mexico, in a freight train carrying nuns and Christian Brothers and priests. He told us that story too.

When I left Louisiana in 1958 to become a Marine lieutenant, I met real southerners, drawling Protestants who had never eaten a crawfish. They told stories. So did everyone else I knew. We were all very young and there were a lot of babies and, often, after parties, some people of both genders spoke with amusement and sometimes derision about the young mothers gathered at one part of a room, talking about babies. Even now, because I have many young friends, and also two very young daughters, I hear this amusement or derision after parties. I confess to taking part in the amusement, now and years ago, in Quantico, Virginia, and Camp Pendleton, California. I was wrong.

The mothers were not talking abstractly about infancy and early childhood. They were telling stories about their children, so that a listener could see and hear and perhaps even smell and touch the child who was not in the room, not even in the house, but at the mother's home, usually in the care of a teenage girl. The mothers were also talking about their motherhood, and to convey those deep emotions and physical and spiritual changes in their lives, they chose what we have always chosen with our friends: they told stories with concrete language, with words that appeal to our senses. We talk abstractly with people whose love or affection or respect we don't want, so we keep them at bay, we do not tell them any of the stories that are part of the collection of stories that is our earthly lives.

In one life, there are so many of these stories and they are so different from each other, that I have come to mistrust a particular sort of novel: the sort that attempts to tell the whole story of a human life or human lives. Unless the novel ends in death, and even then I remain unconvinced: for, with a few magnificent exceptions, those novels by the very nature of their form — they must, finally, end — have left out enough stories to make at least another book.

Years ago, when I believed or at least hoped it would work, I spent some time in marriage counseling. The counseling did not work because it was one last try at keeping two people lovingly in the same home and, unlike baseball and other pursuits, like writing fiction, a last act of will to stay married usually comes too late. What we did in the counselor's office was tell stories. A good counselor won't let you get by with the lack of honesty and commitment we bring to abstractions. And when we told these stories we discovered the truths that were their essence, that were the very reasons we needed to tell the stories; and, like honest fiction writers, we did not know the truth of the stories until we told them. Or, more accurately, until the stories told themselves, took their form and direction from the tactile language of our memory, our pain, and our hope.

Short story writers simply do what human beings have always done. They write stories because they have to; because they cannot rest until they have tried as hard as they can to write the stories. They cannot rest because they are human, and all of us need to speak into the silence of mortality, to interrupt and ever so briefly stop that quiet flow, and with stories try to understand at least some of it.

1986

A SALUTE TO MISTER YATES

RICHARD YATES IS one of our great writers with too few
readers, and no matter how many readers he finally
ends up with, they will still be too few, unless there are
hundreds of thousands in most nations of the world. I have
been his friend for thirty-three years, and he has most often
needed money, and has never complained to me about that,
or about anything else either. For several years in the seven-
ties and eighties, Dick lived in an apartment on Beacon
Street in Boston. It is a street with trees and good old brick
buildings. He lived on the second floor, in two rooms. The
front room was where he wrote and slept. A door at the far
end of it, behind his desk, opened to the kitchen; and adjacent to that was the room I never saw him enter. I suppose
his youngest daughter, Gina, slept there when she came to
visit. Gina's paintings and drawings hung in the first room,
above the bed against one wall, and his desk facing another.
His desk was two tables he placed in the shape of an L;

he sat inside of it, the leg of the L on his right, and a window on his left. Below the window was an alley and parking spaces. On the floor near the kitchen was a small radio, plugged into an outlet; he listened to classical music. The back of a couch was against the long table of the L, and the couch faced the apartment's door, the bathroom, his shelf of books, the closet, and the bed. When I went to visit him I sat on the couch, and he sat on the bed, and we drank Michelob and talked about writing, and writers.

Fluffs of dust were on the floor, and to some eyes that one room where he lived may have looked dirty and cluttered. It was never cluttered. He wrote with a pencil on legal pads; but usually, when I went to see him, he was working on a typed draft, his manual typewriter on the shorter table, before his straight wooden chair; and the typed manuscript stacked on the long table, along with galley proofs and other writers' manuscripts he was reading. His room reminded me of my own bachelor apartments, where I too lived in one room, and rarely entered the other, and my childrens' paintings and drawings hung on the walls: the bed always made, the refrigerator stocked with breakfast food and beer, and every manuscript and book and bit of clothing in place, readily at hand. It was, I believed — and still do — a place that should have been left intact when Dick moved, a place young writers should be able to go to, and sit in, and ask themselves whether or not their commitment to writing had enough heart to live, thirty years later, as Dick did: with time his only luxury, and absolute honesty one of his few rewards.

He woke each morning at seven and ate breakfast, then worked till noon, when he walked perhaps a hundred yards to Massachusetts Avenue, where it intersects with Beacon Street, and across it to a restaurant called The Crossroads.

After lunch he napped, then wrote till evening and returned to The Crossroads for dinner and, even if I ate with him, even if we had dates, he went home around ten o'clock. He did not go to movies, and he never plugged in the television set Penelope Mortimer gave him after she taught at Boston University, then went back to England. It was on the living room floor, facing the couch, its cord lying behind it like a tail.

On Beacon Street now there is only resident parking, but in those days I left my car near Dick's and walked to the Red Sox games. One warm and dry and sunny afternoon, a Saturday in spring, I was walking past The Crossroads, toward Fenway Park, when Dick walked out of the restaurant. He had just eaten lunch and, as always, wore a suit and tie. I have rarely seen him without a tie. I had time before the game for a beer, so we went into The Crossroads and sat in a booth, and I congratulated him on receiving a second Guggenheim grant.

"How much did you get?" I said.

"Well," he said, smiling. "How much did *you* get?"

He was talking about several years earlier, in 1975.

"I asked for twenty," I said. "But I was making eleven-five teaching, so they gave me twelve."

He nodded, his eyes merry.

"The first time," he said, "I got sixty-five hundred. But that was nearly twenty years ago, Andre. This time I got sixteen thousand."

"Sixteen? That's my salary, and I'm having a hard time in Haverhill. Can you make it on sixteen in Boston?"

"Well, Andre," he said, like a man holding a full house in five card stud, "I think I can make it on sixteen thousand dollars."

"You're wonderful," I said. "You're the only writer I

know, your age, who isn't always worrying about money, *talk*ing about money: mortgages and cars and second cars and boats —"

"I don't really think those guys want all that stuff."

"If they gave you a *hun*dred thousand you wouldn't buy a damned thing, would you? You'd live in the same place and write every day and you wouldn't change a *thing*, would you."

"I don't want money," he said. "I just want readers."

1988

Selling Stories

We short story writers are spared some of the major
temptations: we don't make money for ourselves or
anybody else, so the people who make money from writers
leave us alone. No one gives us large advances on stories we
haven't written. I have never envied a writer who makes a
lot of money, because the causal combination of money and
writing frightens me. The act of writing alone is all I can
muster the courage to face in the morning; if my livelihood
and the expectations of publishers depended on it, I doubt
that I could do it at all. So, like the poets, short story writers
live in a safer world. There is no one to sell out to, there
is no one to hurry a manuscript for; our only debt is to
ourselves, and to those stories that speak to us from wherever they live until we write them. And every writer has
stories that only he can give birth to and, until he does, they
float like bodiless spirits crying to be born. I have been
teaching fiction writing to very young students for ten

years, and I am still saddened when one of them leaves a story unborn, before I can hear it all; and, like a nuance of death, I can feel that story and its people drifting away forever.

But that's a different matter, and has to do with confronting oneself at the writing desk, where there are always temptations. When all that is done and the story is in the mail, we don't have to worry about much until someone decides to publish it. Then, with some magazines, we have to do a bit of thinking. I'm forty-one, so I've done a lot of thinking, but I still don't have many answers. Except one: I prefer to publish in quarterlies. That is not the whole truth. I would like to publish in *Harper's* and *Atlantic Monthly*, but I never have, simply because I haven't written anything they liked enough to publish.

For reasons I've forgotten, I used to want to publish in *Esquire*, and there was a time when I mailed stories by special delivery to their fiction editor. Because he had read a story of mine in *Northwest Review* and written to me and said from now on, send everything directly to me. His assistant, a woman I never met but whom I liked anyway, wrote, saying that if the story in *Northwest Review* was one she had rejected, she would apologetically and happily walk through Central Park alone at midnight. This stirred in me memories of one of the sweetest and saddest images of my boyhood: a World War II movie — was it *So Proudly We Hail?* — about nurses or WACs or whatever on an island in the Pacific. Near the end of the movie, one of the girls puts a hand grenade between her breasts, walks into the jungle, and when the Japanese soldiers come out of the brush and surround her, she pulls the pin. That might have been Lana Turner. I wrote the kind woman at *Esquire*, told her she had indeed rejected the story that her boss liked, but *Northwest Review* had taken it and paid for it with a check for ten dollars from the state of Oregon, and she should not walk through that park even at high noon.

But after that I mailed stories to her boss, who rejected them all. This was not disappointing, and if there's anything serious in this piece, here it is, and it's for any young writer who may be reading this and wondering why: In my nineteenth summer I began submitting stories to the *New Yorker, Atlantic Monthly, Harper's, Esquire, Mademoiselle,* the *Saturday Evening Post, Collier's,* through all the commercial magazines, then the quarterlies listed in the back of Foley's *Best American Short Stories.* I knew the stories weren't good enough to be published, but I also knew it was time to enter the game, and by my early twenties I was so used to rejections that they didn't bother me anymore, and they still don't. From magazines, that is. Book publishers are a different story, and there's not room for that one here.

So I wasn't disappointed by the rapid-fire rejections from the man at *Esquire.* But I was confused. Some editors are like lovers, friends, dogs, or roads that one has known for a long time: they are consistent, and I can understand their rejections, even predict them, as after a while you can predict that when the moon is full your friend will go on a tequila drunk and your girl will suddenly cry. The man at *Esquire* had no pattern at all, or perhaps it was one I couldn't figure out. I stopped trying to. For years I had not been able to figure out what the magazine itself was: at times it was serious, at times distasteful, at times silly. I still don't know what it is, and I rarely pay the near-price of a six-pack for it unless it has a sure thing: Cheever or Styron or someone else who is always worth the price, whatever it may be. It would be nice to appear in *Esquire*, but nice finally isn't very much, and one can live peacefully without it.

You see why I say we short story writers live in a safe world. If *Esquire* paid fifty thousand dollars for a story then I might be tempted to learn what their fiction man likes, and what the magazine is really for, or who it is for. The next step would be trying to write what he or they or it likes and that is, of course, one of the many beginnings of one of the many endings of a writer.

And now the *New Yorker*, that magazine hallowed by so many who do not write fiction, and not hallowed by so many who do. Three of my stories have appeared amid their good cartoons and their advertisements for things that exclude all but the rich. This was long ago, and it would be nice to publish there again, because I have four dollars in my savings account, and bills unpaid. Nice, but nothing more. The *New Yorker* frightens me, and I said this to one of its editors, a compassionate man whom I've never met, but who phoned me one night, a night when he was drinking alone, to say he hoped his letter of rejection had not hurt my feelings. When he learned I was sober, or not yet drunk, he told me to make myself a drink; so, standing in my kitchen, I drank several gin gimlets with this good man drinking his scotch in New York, and finally I told him his magazine scared me.

"Scares you? Why?"

"Because you pay so much money."

"We don't pay as much as *TV Guide.* "

"And when there's so much money involved it gets to be very hard to say no to those little changes your boss always wants."

I was referring to the first story they had bought, back in

1967, when they told me I should delete the words "horny," "brown-nose," and "diaphragm." I was young then, less easily angered, more easily impressed, and I deleted the words. It wasn't the money. I had no idea as I cleaned up my manuscript that I would be paid $2,250. When I got the check I was excited, but scared too, and I should have been: for years after that, to this day in fact, as soon as a story I'm working on takes a downward abdominal dip, I say to myself: There goes the *New Yorker*. And I say it with relief, and with that great freedom one feels when writing with no market at all in mind.

Sometimes I buy the *New Yorker*, for the stories and the baseball writing of Roger Angell. But always I am angered while I read it, for I keep seeing those advertisements that bracket the stories. And, since I don't know anyone who reads the *New Yorker* every week or even every month, I can't figure out who does, and why. I can only assume that the publishers know, and that the advertisements are for those people, and in my mind they look very much like the people in the magazine's cartoons. Which is not what really bothers me anyway, since art is for everyone. What angers me is seeing art juxtaposed with advertisements for things which have no use at all except to decorate the body, to turn people into Christmas trees, to turn their vision away from where art is trying to take them.

I have an agent who has become a friend, and I love him as both. Without hyberbole, I can say that he does not make enough money from my work in a year to supply himself with cigarettes. Our arrangement is this: after he has sent a story to as many commercial magazines as he can find, I try the quarterlies. In 1976 he sold a story of mine to *Penthouse* for $1,000. My 90 percent of that pleased me, but I did not laugh all the way to the bank. On the way to the bank is Magee's, the newsstand, variety store, and lunch counter in town, and I stopped for my first look at *Penthouse*. That afternoon I went to see an old friend of mine, who is also an older friend, a philosopher by trade, a man I have gone to through the years for advice.

"Do you think it's immoral to publish in *Penthouse*?" I said.

"I don't think it's immoral to publish anywhere."

"Well, I just looked at it, and they have pictures of cunnilingus."

"That's not cunnilingus. That's a camera angle."

"If you came home and found your wife poised three inches over some guy's mouth, you wouldn't use this kind of casuistry."

"Not me: I'm a voyeur. I'd pull up a chair and watch. What do you care if some guy wants to look at those pictures?"

"I don't. I just don't know if that's any place to put a story. But it's not that simple. The *New Yorker* advertises twenty-five-hundred-dollar gold ballpoints. I don't know if that's any place for a story either."

"You know what your problem is? You *know* how you feel about those gold ballpoints. And in your personal life you're closer to *Penthouse* than you are to gold ballpoints, but you don't want to be public about it. I'd say take their money and forget about it."

So I almost did. I bought a later issue and tried to read it but mostly had to deal with an erection, and I decided the magazine wasn't dumb so much as useless. My story was to appear in August and I didn't get galleys and I began to worry. I was accustomed to small quarterlies that could not afford galleys; their occasional misprints were forgivable. But this was different: among the crotches and the shallowness of the magazine, I wanted badly to preserve the part of myself I had spent on those sentences. For me, there are usually only three pure pleasures that come from writing: finishing a final draft, mailing it, and seeing it in print. And especially with *Penthouse*, I needed to preserve all three. My advance copy arrived; I thumbed past the pictures and found what used to be a story of mine. I went to my desk, laid out the manuscript, and spent a long outraged afternoon reading lines alternately from *Penthouse* and from the typed page. In a sixteen-page manuscript, someone had made eighty-five changes.

The man at the *New Yorker* loves commas more than Henry James did, but he never inserted one without asking my permission. The deleting of "diaphragm," "brown-nose," and "horny" was done with gentle courtesy; perhaps I could have won that one, if I had had the sense to fight. But the *Penthouse* editing, or rewriting, was an intolerable violation, and I wrote a letter to their fiction editor. The letter said a lot of things, and one of them was goodbye to another $900, for he had accepted another story from my agent, though he hadn't paid us yet. When he read the letter he returned the story to my agent, said this is a mass publication, and we don't need writers like that guy. So I don't have to worry about *Penthouse* anymore.

Last winter *Sewanee Review* published a story I had worked on for seventeen months: seven drafts, totaling four hundred pages. The final draft was sixty pages long, and I got $500 for it, and I got that third, necessary, and lovely pleasure: the story, no matter what its worth, has been given a dignity I can see. On those pages it lives alone, untouched by paper genitals, diamonds, and gold.

1977

Marketing

I LOVE SHORT stories because I believe they are the way we live. They are what our friends tell us, in their pain and joy, their passion and rage, their yearning and their cry against injustice. We can sit all night with our friend while he talks about the end of his marriage, and what we finally get is a collection of stories about passion, tenderness, misunderstanding, sorrow, money; those hours and days and moments when he was absolutely married, whether he and his wife were screaming at each other, or sulking about the house, or making love. While his marriage was dying, he was also working, spending evenings with friends, rearing children; but those are other stories. Which is why, days after hearing a painful story by a friend, we see him and say: How are you? We know that by now he may have another story to tell, or he may be in the middle of one, and we hope it is joyful.

This is how we talk to each other, but for some reason

people do not buy collections of short stories. I do, and I take them home and read the first line of each story; then I read them in the order the writer wanted me to. Some books of stories can be read in two or three sittings, like a novel. Others want to be read more slowly, one or two stories an evening, so their effects won't be blurred. Since I was eighteen years old, I wanted a book of my own stories on my shelf. I got it when I was thirty-nine, but before that there were some low-key adventures and comedies.

Some editors wrote that my collection was weak. Those letters were more embarrassing than painful. You can't be hurt because someone doesn't like your work; there will always be someone who doesn't, and very often with good reasons. The rejections which hurt deeply, for they drove me closer to admitting my hope was futile, were the ones that said: If you are writing a novel, or if you have one, or will have one, we will consider publishing these stories, or we will publish these stories. After we have published the novel.

A woman at a publishing house in Boston was one of the kindest and most encouraging editors during that time. For six weeks one summer she held my stories, and I felt they were in caring hands. We wrote letters which became as long and passionate as love letters: about Chekhov and writing and the short story as a form which publishers had to neglect, which she would probably have to neglect too, for she worked at a house that had to make money. No one can blame a publisher for that. So that woman and I had none of the solace that comes when you can rage at someone, can blame them. Like doomed adulterous lovers, we could only share our passion and futility and the wish that our lives had not come to this impasse. And we shared our hope. All this time she was showing the stories to people she worked with, and every Friday afternoon I called her, because the phone was there and the clock was moving toward five and I had to hope that in their last hour of work for the week the publishers had decided to say yes. Then one morning I got her final letter, or the final letter of our summer affair. The people she worked with liked the stories too, but the man at the top said: We can publish them, but what will he do for us?

I sent the stories to a house in New York, and got a letter from its king. He was keeping the stories; but I could not understand, from his letter, whether he meant to publish them. He mentioned a novel, but did not require one. Or did he? Finally I phoned a friend who publishes with that house and has spent much time with its king and I read him the letter.

"Go out and have a drink," he said. "He's publishing your stories."

"What about this novel he mentions? Is he holding the stories in case I have a novel, or is he publishing the stories anyway and he hopes I have a novel, or what?"

"Do you have anything that looks like part of a novel?"

"I have a thirty-five page story."

"Send it to him, and tell him it's the first section of a novel."

"It's a story."

"Look, our business is to get into print, not to worry about being ethical with these mercenary bastards. Send it to him."

So I did, and waited a long time, and finally I called him. He was at lunch, but the woman I spoke to said he had dictated a letter to me that morning.

"What's it say?"

"I don't know. It's still in the machine."

"The machine?"

"You can call about five and I'll read it to you."

I taught my classes that afternoon, or at least went to them, for while I stood in the classroom I saw myself squatting inside a machine in an office in New York. When I called at five, the king came to the phone.

"That piece you sent me looks like a story."

"I guess that's what it is."

"I can't publish your stories." His voice was so wistful that, again, there was no one to blame, no one to scream at. "I mean, I could; but it wouldn't help either of us."

"Why wouldn't it help me?"

"You wouldn't make any money."

"I don't *want* any money. I just want the stories bound on my shelf so they can finally rest and I won't have to worry about them anymore and they won't have to worry about themselves or about me either: you can *have* the stories. I'll give them to you. I just want —"

"No. No, it wouldn't do you any good. If you ever write a novel —"

I spent many evenings during this period lying on my bed and drinking gin and listening to records. When I lost a woman, I played Dylan's songs about losing women. I have found that, in matters like this, the best course is an irrational one: build up some rage, whether it's real or not; think of every flaw she has, multiply it by twenty-three, and, with the help of the juniper berry, convince yourself she is a harridan whose true nature you are only seeing now. On evenings after my book was rejected, I listened to Kris Kristofferson's "To Beat the Devil." Rage had no purpose on those evenings, nor did irrationality. Publishing is a business and you can't dislike a man because he knows his business. So, on my back in body and spirit, I sipped and listened to Kristofferson sing about being in Nashville with songs that no one would hear. When I got out of bed the next morning, my spirit usually got up with me. Good morning, spirit, my old friend; let's keep moving.

In the same circle. In the winter of 1973 I got on that circle for the last time with yet another woman in yet another Boston house. After she read my stories, she invited me to lunch. My oldest daughter has said, about my dining hedonism, that I remember everything that's ever gone into my mouth. But I don't know what I ate that afternoon, or even where. Because I believed that the act of eating lunch with her was a prelude to change. At lunch she talked about the stories, and I think she spoke well of them, but I can't say that with any more certainty than I can recall the restaurant or what I ate. The place was crowded, the woman had a soft voice, and I could not hear what she said. I tried to read her lips. I did not ask her to repeat herself, for I was afraid she would think I wanted a litany of praise. All I could do was nod once in a while. When lunch was over I walked her back to her building, and as we parted, I said: "Which ones don't you like?"

"Oh, I like them all."

She seemed puzzled. Did she think I couldn't handle two Bloody Marys?

"When will I hear from you?" I said.

"Probably next week."

I thanked her and drove home to friends who asked if she had taken the book.

"I don't know," I said. "She has a soft voice."

She had a soft voice in the letter she wrote a week later. It was the same letter I had gotten for years, but there was that voice telling me: This is the way things are, and there is nothing any of us can do about it. She gave me the names of two agents, and said I should not have to keep going through this with publisher after publisher, I should have an agent to receive these letters.

I did not agree. I believed I should perform surgery, sever that book hope once and for all, and learn to live without it. I put the stories in a drawer, told myself they were published in quarterlies anyway, and it was time to be satisfied with that; told myself there was nothing cowardly about leaving this game I could never win; I was lucky to have a life as a teacher and a writer whose stories appeared in quarterlies; it was a life with dignity and I was foolish to need a book on my shelf as testament to it; and many writers would trade circumstances with me in a moment. I still believe all of that, but it was a belief I could not live with, for my dream was stronger than my conviction, my hope stronger than my belief, and eight months later I took the stories out of the drawer. I found the woman's letter and chose the name of one of the agents, only because I liked its sound better, and sent him the stories. He liked them and said he would find a publisher, and I tried not to hope but did anyway, and in spring of the following year he found David Godine of Boston. A year later Godine published the book, and last fall he published another one. Nobody made much money, but the books are on my shelf, and I have a publisher who doesn't talk about novels. And if he never publishes my stories again, it'll be because he doesn't like them, and finally I'll have someone to blame: myself.

Last year a man from New York whispered in my ear; an honest man, a warm and intelligent man, but he whispered about money. His house could do more for me, he said. I told him I wasn't interested. He didn't buy that, so finally he bought a dinner. It was at Ferdinand's in Cambridge, and I had duck and Pouilly-Fuissé.

"What can you do?" I said.

"Give you more money and sell more books."

"Then what? Another book of stories?"

"You'd have to sign a contract promising a novel."

"I write stories."

"So if your next book were a collection of stories, you could use it to break our contract."

"Then what?"

"Go back to Godine."

"I'll stay there. I've been waiting for him since I was eighteen."

1978

Part Four

)-(

Two Ghosts

I AWOKE ON Sunday morning in the house in Provincetown and remembered a woman saying at the party the
night before: *Of course the house is haunted.* She was talking
about the house we were to live in for two weeks: my wife,
our baby daughter, and one of my grown sons. I believe in
ghosts, because I spent some time with one in 1961, so I
asked people about this one. *Sounds,* they said; *sounds in the
night.* I knew what they meant: those sounds which are not
as specifically preternatural as the clanking of chains,
moans from the walls, or screams in the chimney. But the
sounds an old house may or may not make at night, depending on the house, depending on how you are when you
listen to them. One man told us of a couple bringing a small
girl to the house. They had told her nothing about a ghost.
Yet she walked around the room — he didn't say which
room, but I imagine her in the living room — and said:
Ghost; ghost hiding here; ghost.... People told us it was a

benevolent ghost, and I was prepared to believe this too. So that I was not afraid of any mischief from the ghost; I was only, I think, afraid of what I would feel when I first saw it, or did not see it but knew it was there.

It rained or was grey for most of those two weeks, and often there were strong winds. The house is on Commercial Street, faces south, and is across the street from the bay. Our three upstairs bedrooms were at the front of the house, so from their windows we could look between the houses across the street at the water. Our bedrooms were adjacent: the baby, oblivious to ghosts, sea, and the weather on one end, my wife and I on the other, and my grown son in the middle room where the desk was at the window, so my wife wrote there in the mornings, and I worked at it in the afternoons. A hall separated the rooms from two bathrooms, the staircase, and another bedroom. We — I — kept the hall light on so we — I — would not, waking in a strange place with a full bladder, go over the railing and down the stairs. Downstairs is a large living room which should have been comforting but somehow was not: a couch and several good chairs and lamps, my cassette player on the mantelpiece, and a large window facing what would have been the bay but was the house across the street. Still, it was a good place to read.

At night my son, Jeb, was with his new love, my baby daughter slept, and my wife went to bed at a reasonable time, between eleven and twelve, a gift she has. Or so it seems to me, because I cannot do it, and, since quitting sleeping pills in the summer of 1979, I have been able most nights to get to sleep around two. So I spend about three hours a night awake and alone, and that is when, at Provincetown, I heard the sounds.

You've heard them too: the creaking of wood, a sudden

noise like a footfall, and you shiver for an instant, remember it's only wood, and go back to your book. I heard those as I read downstairs, and was frightened, and slowly recovered. But after a few nights I was frightened without noises, and did not recover, and began to read in the wide and very comfortable bed while my wife slept. But sometimes I would go downstairs to smoke. I did not like going downstairs, and this had nothing to do with the sounds, but with the reason for my fleeing upstairs to read: I had begun to sense the ghost's presence. I knew that I sensed it, as I had paid attention to the sounds, because I was thinking about it. I am impressed, often amused, and generally glad that knowing why we feel something so often fails to dispel the feeling. I smoked with fear, and no courage, and was up the stairs again, to the bed, the lamp, and above all, my wife.

One night I woke to the sounds of footsteps on the ceiling above my head; or on the attic floor. I lay there listening, and very soon my wife woke and went to the bathroom. When she came back and got in bed, I said: "Did you hear the ghost walking?"

"That was Jeb going to the bathroom."

"In the attic?" I said, and she went to sleep.

Then one night, still in our first week there, a wind blew hard from the west, from the mainland and across the water, blew against the side of the house opposite our bedrooms. It was a wind that shook trees, and stirred whitecaps out on the bay and, coming through the partly opened bathroom window, pushed open our bedroom door. So when we went to bed, we latched the door: a hook and eye latch on its inside. My wife read for a while, then slept, and I read for two more hours. I was reading Nicolas Freeling then. After a while, the wind died and I was reading paragraphs whose sentences began to merge with lines I had heard spoken during the day, and lines I had thought or was thinking, and images and words that were the beginning of a dream, and I knew that I was nearly asleep, that I actually would sleep, and I turned out the light and did.

There was a bedside clock, an electric one that sat on the window sill at my side of the bed. At three o'clock I suddenly woke. But that is not true: on those nights when I suddenly wake, alert as with adrenaline, it is due to insomnia: whatever that is, wherever in my flesh it exists, it wakes me and either I am poised with energy as though my muscles want nothing less than a session with barbells and dumbbells and a long fast walk, or my body tautens and shifts and turns with the energy of nerves stimulated by too many cups of coffee. That night I was wakened, my body still in the ordinary settled state of one asleep, and only my heart quickening with fear as I turned from my side to my back, pressed my hands against the mattress, and looked across my wife at the sound, the movement, that had wakened me. It was the latch, the hook in the eye. The door did not shut tightly against the doorjamb, so a vertical line of light from the hall was visible between them. In this light I could clearly see the hook moving back and forth with the rapidity of the sound, the metallic click click click, that had startled me from sleep.

My wife is far more sensitive to noise than I am, and needs silence, or what we can have of it, both to go to sleep and stay asleep; while, usually, noise neither keeps me awake nor bothers me when I do sleep. But, as the hook clicked fast against the outer rim of the eye, as though pushed and pulled back and forth, she slept. In that thin line of light, I watched the hook, breathed deeply, pressed legs as well as my hands into the mattress, and said, in my mind: *All right. Come on in. Let's see what you look like.* I do not know how long I waited. More than a few seconds; probably no more than two minutes. Then the hook sprang up from the eye, and fell free. The door slowly swung open, admitting more light from the hall; after an opening of six or eight inches, it stopped. Nothing entered. Nor did any wind. The door simply stood ajar, and the house was silent, as were the trees outside the window. After a while my heart calmed, and I slept.

Next morning I did not tell the family. My wife not only is able to sleep early, but also she cannot stay up late, so at Provincetown, as at home, there were nights when I stayed out with people while she went home, and I did not want her knowing about the latch, then having to sleep alone. Probably, too, I wished to avoid the responsibility of going home early, or the guilt of staying out.

But on Saturday night, a week after we had arrived, we went out before and after a fiction reading, then she took the sitter home, and I went up to our bedroom and shut the door, as it had been that night, not flush with the jamb, but pushed against it. I put the hook in the eye. Then I pulled the door toward me, as though wind were pushing it open. I did it slowly, gently. When the door touched the hook, it moved against the outer rim of the eye. I grasped it with finger and thumb, and tried to move it back and forth, to shake it click click clicking. It would not move. The door pulled against it kept it still, pressed against the outer side of the eye. I shoved the door against the jamb, then the hook was loose in the eye. I could move it and make the sound I had heard, had watched that night.

I did this several times, pulling the door against the hook with varying degrees of force, trying then to move the hook, and each time I could not. So I shut the door, as well as it would shut, always with that thin crack between it and the jamb, and saw finally what I had already known but had to demonstrate to myself anyway: that the only way the wind could have opened the latch was to come through the bathroom and hall, to come like a vertical, thin blade, a wind moving through space only the size of the crack, so that, without touching the door and moving it against the hook, it would go unimpeded through that crack, with only the hook in its path. There had not been any wind, at that hour, that night, and I knew it, but wanted to consider whatever physical causes there may have been, no matter how improbable or absurd they may seem. For, though I believe in ghosts, they still seem nearly as improbable as a narrow shaft of wind crossing Provincetown from west to east, slipping between the door and the wall, and opening the latch on its way through our bedroom. And they seem nearly as improbable as a wind that could somehow shake and lift a hook jammed tightly against its eye, and then only open the door a matter of inches, rather than pushing it completely open.

But only nearly, so I then walked through the house, into each of the rooms, starting where Cadence, our baby daughter, slept, and spoke aloud and gently to the ghost, said that I knew it was there, I believed in it and did not require a further manifestation, but that if it wished to continue, I hoped and asked it please not to disturb my wife or baby; and that if there were something it needed, or something it wished done, I would gladly do it.

When my wife returned, I told her all of it, and she believed it but was not afraid, so I left and went to the party up the street. We were there one more week, and the ghost was quiet, and we told the story to people. Many, of course, said it was the wind.

But there was no wind in my stateroom aboard the *USS*

Ranger, moored at Yokosuka, Japan, in late September of 1961. I was a first lieutenant in the Marine Corps, serving a year of sea duty with the Marine Detachment aboard the aircraft carrier, a large ship weighing seventy thousand tons, with a flight deck a thousand feet long. I mention this to help explain my feelings that night. In the ship's crew were thirty-five hundred men; added to that number were the squadrons which were aboard the *Ranger* for its seven-month deployment. So every day, as in a town, you saw faces you had never seen before.

I had never seen his. He appeared at four o'clock on a Monday morning. I was in the duty section on Sunday and, though I was not assigned Officer of the Deck watch that day, I had to stay aboard. I'm sure I went to Mass in the forecastle, and probably I worked on a novella I was writing then, and wrote to my wife, and read. Perhaps I watched a movie, in the afternoon, in the Marine Barracks. It was beneath the ship's bakery, and every morning we smelled bread baking, then a Marine would come down the ladder with fresh, hot loaves. In those days I slept at will, and at ten o'clock that Sunday night I climbed into my bunk, and slept.

On the *Ranger,* junior officers shared a stateroom, and lieutenant-commanders and above, and my skipper, a Marine captain, had single rooms. My roommate was not only a practicing southern Baptist, but was between six feet four and six and a half feet tall, and weighed in the range of two hundred thirty to two hundred fifty pounds. He had those qualities I have so often encountered in devout southern Baptists: he did not smoke, he rarely spoke profanely, but at times he had about him the righteousness of a leader of a lynch mob. Once, though, during those seven months in the Western Pacific, he did come aboard drunk from liberty, and frightened me more than the visitor who appeared that night at Yokosuka. I was asleep in the upper bunk, whose mattress was level with his pectoral muscles; he stood at my bunk, said: *I'm drunk, roomie,* and with a foolish grin, he grasped my shorts in one fist, my T-shirt in the other, and lifted me, held me suspended, horizontal above my bed. That Sunday night he was ashore, and now I wish he had been in the room, in his lower bunk, so my memory of this would be comic. But perhaps he would have slept, as my wife did in Provincetown while the latch announced a visit. Surely, though, I would have waked him; and he would either have seen the ghost, or seen me pointing to it, and what would have followed would be a better story.

But he was in Yokosuka and, late as it was, I know he was chastely and soberly in Yokosuka (some men did that, simply spent a night in a hotel, to be away from the ship), and I was asleep, the bulkhead on my left, our spacious stateroom on my right. It had two desks, adjacent and facing a bulkhead, and next to them were our two wall lockers, and then the bunks. Opposite the desks were a lavatory and mirror. Filipino stewards did motel maid service every day, and picked up our laundry outside our door, and placed it, folded and wrapped in paper, on our bunks when it was done. We each had a shelf alongside the bulkhead next to our mattresses, and reading lamps over our pillows. On my shelf I kept an ashtray, books, and a small alarm clock, whose numbers and hands glowed at me in the dark. At four o'clock Monday morning, I was suddenly awake.

The first thing I looked at was not the clock. For I woke as you wake when someone comes into your room and stands over your bed, looking at you. I was lying on my back, and I turned my head to the right, and looked into his face. It was swaying from side to side, with the rest of his body, and on it was a grin as foolish as the one I would see months later as my roommate lifted me into the air as though I were a two-by-four. His face appeared bloated by recent heavy drinking. His hair was dry, light brown, and brushed or combed with a part on the left side. He wore a sport jacket, or perhaps the coat of a suit; I believe it was tweed. He had a button-down pale blue shirt, its collar open, and beneath that small unbuttoned V was a dark knit tie, its knot pulled down from his throat. My fright was quick, and I sat up, probably with no help from my hands or arms. Then, as suddenly, I realized that he was simply a Naval officer I had never seen before (officers were required to wear civilian clothes ashore, if they left the confines of Naval bases), he was very drunk, was in not only the wrong room but the wrong area of the ship, and I would have to get up and dress and help him to his room, keep him from injury or death on the steep ladders of our huge home. I glanced away from him, to turn on the reading lamp, and when I looked again, he was not there. So he had fallen to the deck. It did not occur to me to wonder about a fall so silent. I peered over the side of my bunk, and the deck was as empty as the space he had just filled.

That was when I looked at the clock, then spoke to myself, in my mind, but with sentences. Usually, when I talk to myself, it is with images, and pieces of sentences. When I do actually use the language, in the form of a monologue, I address it to someone I love. Sometimes these become dialogues. But, as well as I know, I only address myself when I need encouragement: to get out of bed, or to get in it and try to sleep, or to start a workout or complete one when I feel I can't, or to go to the desk and write. That night I said to myself: *It is four o'clock. You have been asleep for six hours.* Then I pinched the flesh on my forearm. *You are awake.* I turned off the light and, immediately, before I could lie back and settle on the pillow, he was there.

I turned on the light, and sat there on the bunk looking at the room, empty save for our wall lockers, our desks, our lavatory and mirror. By then, my bladder wanted relief, and I suppose now it was the ghost who caused that. But this is also the time to make clear that, save for the first time I saw him, and the first time he disappeared, and the second time I saw him, I felt no fear for the rest of the night. I am as frightened of bedroom intruders in the night as the next person, whether the intruder is mortal or not, so this was not a matter of insouciance in the face of physical danger or simply fear. I have of course thought much about that night, from time to time in the past twenty-two years, and my only answer is this: the ghost did not mean to frighten me, but meant instead to convey his own need. For when I first saw him, then quickly saw him again, swaying drunkenly, with that grin widening into his bloated cheeks, he made me want to help him find the way to his room. He looked only young and friendly and absolutely helpless.

I climbed down from my bunk. The room was well-lit by my reading lamp, and I stepped into the passageway, which was always darkened, and lit only by red lights placed at certain points, close enough so there was always light, but little of it. The light was red to protect pilots' night vision. The passageway between our room and the head was L-shaped. A red light was at the first corner and, as I turned it, I saw him walking toward me. He swayed, he grinned, his face and his very posture told me he was lost, and unable to gain his wits. I stopped and waited. I do not know whether he wore a sport jacket or a suit because I could not look away from his face. I had a question for him, and it was not one I considered, thought about, but one that came to me as naturally as true questions do. I wanted to ask him: *What do you want?* So I stood waiting, and when he reached me he stopped, and we faced each other in the dark, and the dim red light. I looked at his face. When I opened my mouth to speak, he vanished.

I went on to the head, whose door was closed and inside was lighted, and stood at the urinal, watching my urine, and still did not think *ghost,* did not think anything at all, but simply stood there in some state that was not anxiety, and certainly not peace, but excited curiosity, and wonder. I returned to the stateroom.

What would I have done, had he come howling at four o'clock into my room, turned on the water faucets, taken my pen and written on my manuscript, sent the wall lockers flying? You know as well as I do, for it can only be imagined: my fleeing in skivvies down passageways, my crewcut turned white — But he did none of this to me, and I know that is why I slept again. Not at once, though. I climbed into my bunk, looked around the room, then lay on my back, pulled up the sheet and blanket (the ship was air-conditioned too; there are much worse ways to serve), smoked a cigarette, then turned out the light. In the dark he swayed and grinned beside me. I turned on the lamp, and he was gone. I left on the lamp, turned my back to the room, my face to the bulkhead, and slept.

That fall and winter we tied up at Yokosuka, for a week or so of liberty, many times, more than at any other port. He did not come back. Or, if he did, he came while I was ashore, and did not waken my roommate. Or he came again while I slept, and chose not to disturb me. Perhaps by then he knew I could not help him.

1985

INTENSIVE CARE

That fourth of July night in the hospital in Montpelier, Vermont, I listened to the Red Sox playing in Fenway Park. Twilight's brushstrokes of color were low on the horizon, and the trees and foothills were dark but still green. Then it was dusk, then night, and the Red Sox had won. Downstairs at the main desk you lied, old friend Dave Supple, and told them you were my brother.

So you could come up to my room in intensive care and smile down at my smile under the oxygen tubes in my nostrils and, quickly as the professional bartender you are, glance at and absorb without weakening your smile or glazing your eyes the tube going into a vein in my left wrist and the twin wires rising from my bare chest to the heart monitor. It was to my right, above and between us, the screen and the lighted waves. You shook my hand, and I said: "Remember: it's *you* who wants to be placed like a Cheyenne in a tree. I want my ashes buried among the poplars on my hill."

You blushed and said: "Aw, come on."

I did not tell you that my true wish was as illegal as yours. Two days later your wife and I devised a way to steal you from casket and funeral home the night before your burial, drive you out into the northern California boondocks, put you in a tree, and keep ourselves out of jail. I do not want to be cremated. In our country there is no pyre, and I would not leave my family without a ritual while they wait for the urn. I imagine them drinking at a bar, looking at their watches, knowing a good bar clock is always fast. Strange, Dave: some scorn funerals, say they are for the living. I agree, and celebrate that; yet you and I have planned and lived our funerals too. Three nights before the hospital, I turned to you at Fenway Park and said: *We always God-damnit have fun.*

You stood on my right and we talked about the ball game and young Jeff Sellers pitching and picking up the win. Father and husband and writer by day, your night work behind the bar has given you the talents of a detective, a spy, a thief: before leaving, you looked again in an instant at the tubes, the monitor. Then still smiling you strongly shook my hand and said: "Well, smoke filtereds and keep the salt off the rim."

We laughed, and as you walked away I called to your back at the door: "Goodnight, Brother."

"What?" you said, over your shoulder; and then: "Oh. Right. Goodnight, Brother."

In the morning the cardiologist said it was not my heart, only fatigue, and a week later I knew that you and I had received a gift. For one of us will answer a telephone then travel to a funeral; or perhaps the theft of a dead friend, and a night drive into the country. But we've had our deathbed farewell, and now I know that it doesn't matter which friend is on his feet. The goodbye is the same.

On Sunday in Montpelier, with wives and friends and my young daughter, we all laughed through a long breakfast at a restaurant counter, and I believe my heart knew then what I could not articulate for another six days: knew that in the hospital our love became *was,* so you drove from there to the bar and shots of tequila, and now it will never be *was* again. It is, and I have already with your wife placed you on boards in the tree, and you have found a way to bury me whole in my spot of the earth.

1986

LIGHTS OF THE LONG NIGHT

I REMEMBER THE headlights, but I do not remember the car hitting Luis Santiago and me, and I do not remember the sounds our bodies made. Luis died, either in the ambulance, or later that night in the hospital. He was twenty-three years old. I do not remember leaving the ground my two legs stood on for the last instant in my life, then moving through the air, over the car's hood and windshield and roof, and falling on its trunk. I remember lying on my back on that trunk and asking someone: *What happened?*

I did not lose consciousness. The car did not injure my head or my neck or my spine. It broke my right hand and scraped both arms near my wrists, so my wife believes I covered my face with my arms as I fell. I lay for a while on the trunk, talking to a young man, then to a woman who is a state trooper, then I was in an ambulance, stopped on the highway, talking to a state trooper, a man, while he cut my trousers and my right western boot. That morning my wife saw the left boot on the side of the highway, while she was driving home from the hospital in Boston. The car had knocked it off my foot. The state troopers got the boot for my wife, but I did not leave the hospital with a left foot or, below the middle of my knee, a left leg.

While the state trooper was cutting and we were talking, I saw Luis Santiago on a stretcher. People were putting him into an ambulance. Lying in the ambulance and watching Luis I knew something terrible had happened and I said to the trooper: *Did that guy die?* I do not remember what the trooper said, but I knew then that Luis was either dead or soon would be. Then I went by ambulance to a clinic in Wilmington where Dr. Wayne Sharaf saved my life, and my wife Peggy and my son Jeb were there, then an ambulance took me to Massachusetts General Hospital in Boston, where they operated on me for twelve hours.

Luis Santiago said what were probably his last words on earth to me: *Por favor, señor, please help, no hablo Ingles.* This was around one o'clock in the morning of 23 July 1986. I was driving north on Route 93, going from Boston to my home in Haverhill, Massachusetts. The highway has four lanes and I was driving in the third. That stretch of road is straight and the visibility on 23 July was very good, so when I saw the Santiagos' car I did not have to apply the brakes or make any other sudden motions. It was ahead of me, stopped in the third lane, its tail lights darkened. I slowed my car. To the right of the Santiagos' car, in the break-down lane, a car was parked and, behind it, a woman stood talking into the emergency call box. Her back was to me. I was driving a standard shift Subaru, and I shifted down to third, then second, and drove to the left, into the speed lane, so I could pass the left side of the Santiagos' car and look into it for a driver, and see whether or not the driver was hurt. There were no cars behind me. Luz Santiago stood beside the car, at the door to the driver's side, and her forehead was bleeding and she was crying. I drove to the left side of the road and parked near the guard rail and turned on my emergency blinker lights. Because of the guard rail, part of my car was still in the speed lane. I left the car and walked back to Luz Santiago. She was still crying and bleeding and she asked me to help her. She said: *There's a motorcycle under my car.*

I looked down. Dark liquid flowed from under her engine and formed a pool on the highway, and I imagined a motorcycle under there and a man dead and crushed between the motorcycle and the engine and I knew I would have to look at him. Then, for the first time, I saw Luis Santiago. He came from the passenger's side, circling the rear of the car, and walked up to me and Luz, standing beside the driver's door and the pool of what I believed was blood on the pavement. Later I learned that it was oil from the crankcase and the abandoned motorcycle Luz had run over was no longer under her car. Luis was Luz's brother and he was young and I believe his chest and shoulders were broad. He stopped short of Luz, so that she stood between us. That is when he spoke to me, mostly in his native tongue, learned in Puerto Rico.

I do not remember what I said to him, or to Luz. But I know what I was feeling, thinking: first I had to get Luz off the highway and lie her down and raise her legs and cover her with my jacket, for I believed she was in danger of shock. Then I would leave Luis with Luz and return to her car and look under its engine at the crushed man. We left her car and walked across the speed lane to the left side of the highway. We did not have to hurry. No cars were coming. We walked in column: I was in front, Luz was behind me, and Luis was in the rear. At the side of the road we stopped. I saw headlights coming north, toward us. We were not in danger then. If we had known the car was going to swerve toward us, we could have stepped over the guard rail. I waved at the headlights, the driver, my raised arms crossing in front of my face. I wanted the driver to stop and help us. I wanted the driver to be with me when I looked under Luz's car. We were standing abreast, looking at the car. I was on the right, near the guard rail; Luz was in the middle, and Luis stood on her left. I was still waving at the car when it came too fast to Luz's car and the driver swerved left, into the speed lane, toward my Subaru's blinking emergency lights, and toward us. Then I was lying on the car's trunk and asking someone: *What happened?*

Only Luis Santiago knows. While I was in Massachusetts General Hospital my wife told me that Luz Santiago told our lawyer I had pushed her away from the car. I knew it was true. Maybe because my left thigh was the only part of my two legs that did not break, and because the car broke my right hip. When the car hit us, Luis was facing its passenger side, Luz was between its headlights, and I was facing the driver. In the hospital I assumed that I had grabbed Luz with my left hand and jerked and threw her behind me and to my right, onto the side of the highway. That motion would have turned my body enough to the left to protect my left thigh, and expose my right hip to the car. But I do not think the patterns of my wounds told me I had pushed Luz. I knew, from the first moments in the stationary ambulance, that a car struck me because I was standing where I should have been; and, some time later, in the hospital, I knew I had chosen to stand there, rather than leap toward the guard rail.

On 17 September 1986 I left the hospital and came home.

In December, Dr. Wayne Sharaf talked to me on the phone. He is young, and he told me I was the first person whose life he had saved, when he worked on me at the clinic in Wilmington. Then he said that, after working on me, he worked on Luz Santiago, and she told him I had pushed her away from the car. I thanked him for saving my life and telling me what Luz had told him. I said: *Now I can never be angry at myself for stopping that night.* He said: *Don't ever be. You saved that woman's life.* Perhaps not. She may have survived, as I have. I am forever a cripple, but I am alive, and I am a father and a husband, and in 1987 I am sitting in the sunlight of June and writing this.

1987

SKETCHES AT HOME

10 December 1986

So MANY OF the nurses did this so frequently that I believe they are taught to do it. You ask for something: a pitcher of iced water, a cup of juice. The nurse is friendly, even affectionate: Sure, Andre; can I get you anything else? She leaves. Her return is usually not quick. She has other patients. Then she comes into the room, and to your bed. I always thought of it as the room, and only sometimes my bed. She places the pitcher or the cup of juice on the wheeled table beside the bed. There is another affectionate exchange: she announces your beverage or apologizes for taking so long and you thank her, and you mean it too. She is friendly and competent and you could not get through the hours without her — you could survive, but it would be terrible — and you are more thirsty than you ever were outside the hospital, save after a long workout in hot weather. She leaves. You reach for the pitcher or cup and do not touch it. You roll toward the table and extend your arm; if you are in traction you cannot truly roll; you just turn a bit. You still cannot touch the plastic pitcher or paper cup. With one hand you hold the table and pull it toward you, then turn it this way or that until its angle brings your drink closer. Finally you can touch the side of the vessel, carefully turn it in a series of partial circles until it is within range. Then you hold it and pour from it or bring it to your lips. This is also true of the small paper container that holds your pills. The nurses place them, too, just out of reach. Not every time, but enough of the time, enough. Hospital challenge.

Today is the tenth of December, nineteen eighty-six. Exactly twenty-five years ago I finished the first draft of a novella called *One Face in the Morning;* I was a first lieutenant, executive officer of the Marine Detachment aboard the carrier *USS Ranger.* Today at home in a hospital bed I phoned the Phoenix Bookstore in Haverhill and spoke to my friend, Jack Herlihy, who is the store's co-owner. I asked him to order Thomas McGuane's book of stories; he already had it at the store. We bantered for a while, then he said someone had just come in and was fondling one of my books and wanted to tell me hello. It was the doctor who treated me at the hospital in Wilmington, north of Boston and a short distance south of the place on Route 93 where, on 23 July, the car hit me and Mr. Santiago, who died soon afterward, that night. They worked on me at Wilmington a. d that is where my wife, Peggy, and my son, Jeb, first saw me. On the phone, the doctor told me they saved my life at Wilmington, then sent me to Massachusetts General. So in my December bed at home I asked him what I was like: Was

I bleeding a lot? Screaming? I was not bleeding so much, he said, but I was in shock and they put inflatable pants on me. I said I remembered the sound of them, but nothing else. He said they were to bring up my blood pressure; it was the shock I was in. And no, I wasn't screaming. I was talking. I told them a lot about the accident. (Shock kept me for a while from pain; I do not remember when the one left, and the other moved in.) The doctor said on the phone: The other fellow passed on, as you know. But you saved the woman's life. I asked him if I told him that in the clinic at Wilmington. No, he said, it came out in the wash later on. She told me. I was with her all night. (It was her brother the car killed. He was visiting her from Puerto Rico. On the highway, standing beside their car that had struck an abandoned motorcycle, he said to me: *Señor, por favor, please help, no hablo Ingles.* That is all he said to me.) I told the doctor the woman had told my lawyer someone pulled her out of the way; she could not remember who. I had suspected and hoped I had done it: she stood between her brother and me and he was in line with the passenger side of the car that hit us, so he was near the center of the road; I was in front of the driver's side and near the edge of the road; when the car hit us, she was on the ground beside the road. No, the doctor said, that night she said you pulled her out of the way. So you saved a life that night. I said: So did you. Yes, he said. I told him I would like to buy him a drink. I had never, I said, bought a drink for anyone who had saved my life. I told him at Massachusetts General a male nurse and a doctor had saved my life one night when an artery burst in my lower left leg, before it was amputated, but I was in the hospital for a long time after that and could not buy them a drink. Then I told him why I had wanted to be the one who had saved the woman: because now that I was certain, I could never be angry at myself for stopping and going out on the highway to them, and their car. Yes, the doctor said, J know.

12 December 1986

Yesterday, 11 December, Cadence became four years and six months old. A week ago she came home from play school after dark, as she often does these short December days. I lay in my hospital bed in the small library at the west end of the house. At the other end I could hear Peggy and Cadence talking. Nearly always Cadence comes into the house talking. She said: "I'm going to watch Disaney."

There was something not childish about the way she said it. I imagined her taking off her coat as she spoke. She came down the hall to talk to me. At home we only let her watch *Sesame Street, Mister Rogers,* VCR cartoons. That night we had no cartoon for her because the woman who runs play school had told her about Disney. At six o'clock she climbed onto my bed and I turned on the television with remote control, and with another control switch raised the head of the bed so Cadence could see the screen above my right foot in its cast; the entire leg was in a cast, and covered by a green camouflage-covered poncho liner a Marine major gave me. First Mickey Mouse was on the screen. Cadence lay touching my side, her head on my shoulder; my arm was around her.

But they were showing *Davy Crockett* with Fess Parker. Cadence said: This isn't Disaney. I explained to her why it was Disney, and told her I did not understand why they were showing it at six o'clock, when kids would be watching. Often Cadence cries suddenly when she is disappointed but she did not. *Crockett* was boring, but we watched it anyway, and soon she was restless and talking. Now and then she voiced her objection to Davy Crockett in general. But she was calm and when Crockett ended she climbed down from the raised head of the bed, which she likes to do, then went to talk to Peggy in the kitchen.

I was not calm. It has been a week now, almost to the hour, but I still recall it with sorrow. This is not a sad memory for me because Cadence did not enjoy something on television. No: it is because in her voice that day I heard something for the first time. When she said in the kitchen across the house from me *I'm going to watch Disaney,* her tone was different. It was not one of those common to her: excitement, delight, happy anticipation. It was an announcement, and its tone, though high-pitched, was that of an adult at the end of a day saying: *I'm going to take a long shower* or *I'm going to have a martini* or *We're going out to dinner.* So remembering, I am sad, thinking of all the disappointments and betrayals and horrors waiting for her out there, after her happy instincts and announcements as a grown woman.

One night in the hospital I was lying with the light off, and I needed something. Maybe morphine or juice or water. I was about to press the button for a nurse when down the hall an old woman began to scream. She did not stop and the screams did not diminish in volume; they had the energy of her pain. I did not press the button. I thought: you cannot ask for something when someone else is in pain. Then I thought: But there is always someone suffering, so I should never ask for anything. And at once I knew a saint would take that idea and run with it, would live that way. I waited until the nurse cared for the woman and she stopped screaming, then I pressed the button.

2 January 1987

I call them the terrors but they are not bad. I returned home from the hospital on 17 September and a few days later they began, and they have stayed. Every day at sundown I become afraid. Now on 2 January 1987 I have been afraid throughout the day, and this has been going on for over a week. The road that night comes back to me, the lights of the car, the hospital. I see Luz Santiago sitting beside the road while the car hits her brother and me. I of course did not see her; I threw her there; witnesses say that is where she was.

But I am afraid of more than memory: I am afraid of death, my own and that of everyone I love: and injury, to me and everyone I love. I am most afraid for the physically weakest, Cadence, and today when Peggy wheeled me from my bed to the dining room for lunch, I saw one of Cadence's music boxes on the table and at once thought of seeing it with her gone, with her dead, and then tears were on my cheeks and I took a Xanax, a tranquilizer.

I think often of soldiers, especially those from Vietnam because it is more recent. I wonder if my fear is like theirs, with the same causes, and I know their experience was worse, because I was not in a war but struck in an instant during a peaceful summer, then was in a hospital near home, and my family and friends were with me. Some veterans have told me of their fear long after their wars.

From my bed now the world is a frightful place of death and pain and sorrow. We must love soldiers who have fought. Their nationality does not matter; their very characters do not. We must love them because of what they suffered, the terrible things done to them and to their comrades; and some of them have done terrible things too. I was a Marine officer in peacetime. Today, reading James Kennaway's wonderful *Tunes of Glory,* I remembered how deeply I loved my troops. I thought of landmines in Vietnam. I thought of watching my troops being killed or injured. And I believed it possible that I could force Vietnamese peasants to walk through an area we were afraid was mined; and that if it were possible for me to do such a thing, it would be out of love for my men, and that I would know I was committing terrible and unforgivable murder, because war is terrible and unforgivable.

23 May 1988

Twenty-two months to the day since the car hit me. A year ago, in May, with much prayer, I forgave its driver. I have read a lot about Vietnam since January of 1987, and I have talked with two close friends who were Marines there. I am still in a wheelchair, but I have very little physical pain now, and the fear is gone. So my soul is not as fragile and I know now that even war is forgivable, as all human actions can be, ought to be. After the dead are buried, and the maimed have left the hospitals and started their new lives, after the physical pain of grief has become, with time, a permanent wound in the soul, a sorrow that will last as long as the body does, after the horrors become nightmares and sudden daylight memories, then comes the transcendent and common bond of human suffering, and with that comes forgiveness, and with forgiveness comes love, even for the men who in suits and ties start and end wars, but most of all for the soldiers, whether at Borodino or Gettysburg or Hue, who fought and died and lost arms and legs and sight and hearing and kinetic muscles and functioning brains and remained physically whole but were never again able to love with wholeness another human being: those young soldiers who fought not for ideas but because they loved one another with a greater love than nearly all we civilians ever witness, ever give.

1986/1988

A Woman in April

I N NEW YORK CITY, the twenty-fifth of April 1988 was a
warm and blue day, and daylight savings time held the
sun in the sky after dinner and all the way from the restaurant to Lincoln Center, where we were supposed to be at
eight o'clock. The way from the restaurant to Lincoln Center was sidewalks, nearly all of them with curbs and no
curb cuts, and streets with traffic; and we were with my
friend David Novak, and my friend and agent, Philip
Spitzer, pushing my wheelchair and pulling it up curbs and
easing it down them while I watched the grills and wind-
shields of cars. I call David the Skipper because he was a
Marine lieutenant then captain in Vietnam and led troops
in combat, so I defer to his rank, although I was a peacetime
captain while he was still a civilian. Philip is the brother I
never had by blood.

Philip of course lives in New York. I happily do not.
Neither does the Skipper. He lives here in Massachusetts,

and he and his wife drove to New York that day, a Monday, and my daughter Suzanne and son Andre and friends and I came in two more cars, because Andre and I were reading that night at Lincoln Center with Mary Morris and Diana Davenport. In Massachusetts we had very little sun and warmth during the spring, and that afternoon, somewhere in Connecticut, we drove into sunlight, and soon the trees along the road were green with leaves. We had not seen those either at home, only the promise of buds.

At close to eight o'clock the sky was still blue and the Skipper pushed me across the final street, then turned my chair and leaned it backward and pulled it up steps to the Plaza outside the Center. We began crossing the greyish white concrete floor and, as Philip spoke and pointed up, I looked at the tall buildings flanking the Plaza, angles of grey-white, of city color, against the sky, deepening now, but not much, still the bright blue of spring after such a long winter of short days, lived in bed, in the wheelchair, in physical therapy, in the courthouse losing my wife and two little girls. Philip told us of a Frenchman last year tightrope walking across the space between these buildings, without a net.

Then I looked at the people walking on the Plaza. My only good memories of New York are watching people walk on the streets, and watching people in bars and restaurants, and some meals or drinks with friends, and being with Philip. But one summer I spent five days with him and for the first time truly saw the homeless day after day and night after night, and from then on, whenever I went there, I knew the New York I was in, the penthouses and apartments and cabs and restaurants, were not New York, anymore than the Czar's Russia was the Russia of Chekhov's freed serfs, with their hopes destroyed long before they were born. Still on that spring Monday I loved watching the faces on the Plaza.

Like Boston, New York has beautiful women to look at, though in New York the women, in general, are made up more harshly, and they dress more self-consciously; there is something insular about their cosmetics and clothing, as if they have come to believe that sitting at a mirror with brushes and tubes and vials, and putting on a dress of a certain cut and color starts them on the long march to spiritual fulfillment with a second wind. And in New York the women walk as though in the rain; in Boston many women stroll. But then most New Yorkers walk like people in rain, leaving the stroll to police officers, hookers, beggars and wandering homeless, and teenagers who are yet unharried by whatever preoccupations preoccupy so many from their driving preoccupation with loneliness and death.

Women were on the Plaza, their pace slower as they neared the building, and looking to my right I saw a lovely one. She could have been thirty, or five years on either side of it. She wore a dark brown miniskirt, or perhaps it was black; I saw it and her strong legs in net stockings for only a moment, because they were in my natural field of vision from my chair. But a woman's face is what I love. She was in profile and had soft thick brown hair swaying at her shoulders as she strode with purpose but not hurry, only grace. She was about forty feet away, enough distance so that, when I looked up, I saw her face against the sky.

"Skipper," I said. "Accidently push me into *her.*"

The forward motion of her legs and arms did not pause, but she immediately turned to me and, as immediately, her lips spread in a smile, and her face softened with it, and her eyes did, all at once from a sudden release in her heart that was soft too in her voice: "I heard that."

She veered toward me, smiling still, with brightened eyes.

"It was a compliment," I said.

The Skipper was pushing my chair, Philip was beside me, and she was coming closer. Then she said: "I know."

She angled back to her first path, as though it were painted there for her to follow, and Philip said: "That *never* happens in New York."

"It's the wheelchair," I said. "I'm harmless."

But I knew that was not true. There was no time to explain it then, and anyway I wanted to hold her gift for a while before giving it away with words.

Living in the world as a cripple allows you to see more clearly the crippled hearts of some people whose bodies are whole and sound. All of us, from time to time, suffer this crippling. Some suffer it daily and nightly; and while most of us, nearly all of us, have compassion and love in our hearts, we cannot or will not see these barely visible wounds of other human beings, and so cannot or will not pick up the telephone or travel to someone's home or write a note or make some other seemingly trifling gesture to give to someone what only we, and God, can give: an hour's respite, or a day's, or a night's; and sometimes more than respite: sometimes joy.

Yet in a city whose very sidewalks show the failure of love, the failure to make agape a bureaucracy, a young woman turned to me with instinctive anger or pride, and seeing me in a wheelchair she at once felt not pity but lighthearted compassion. For seeing one of her kind wounded, she lay down the shield and sword she had learned to carry (*I dried my tears/ And armed my fears/ With ten thousand/ shields and spears*, William Blake wrote), and with the light of the sun between us, ten or fifteen feet between us, her face and voice embraced me.

For there is a universality to a wounded person: again and again, for nearly two years, my body has drawn sudden tenderness from men and women I have seen for only those moments in their lives when they helped me with their hands or their whole bodies or only their eyes and lips and tongues. They see, in their short time with me, a man injured, as they could be; a man always needing the care of others, as they could too. Only the children stare with frightened curiosity, as they do at funeral processions and the spoken news of death, for they know in their hearts that they too will die, and they believe they will grow up and marry and have children, but they cannot yet believe they will die.

But I am a particular kind of cripple. In New York I was not sitting on a sidewalk, my back against a wall, and decades of misfortune and suffering in my heart. I was not wearing dirty clothes on an unwashed body. Philip and the Skipper wore suits and ties. I rode in a nine-hundred-dollar wheelchair, and rolled across the Plaza at Lincoln Center. Yet I do not ask that woman, on seeing my body, to be struck there in the sunlight, to stand absolutely still and silent and hear like rushing tide the voices of all who suffer in body and in spirit and in both, then to turn before my dazzled eyes and go back to her home and begin next morning to live as Mother Teresa, as Dorothy Day. No: she is one of us, and what she said and did on that April evening was, like the warm sunlit sky, enough: for me, for the end of winter, for the infinite possibilities of the human heart.

1988

BASTILLE DAY

EARLY IN THE morning in Louisiana in 1963, on the four-teenth of July, my father died. He left me forks and spoons made in New Orleans of silver coins from the court of the queen who said: *Let them eat cake;* and a sword an ancestor had worn or wielded or never touched on Bastille Day; and a Colt .41 revolver his own father's death had released to him; and the watch I slid from his wrist before they came to his house, his bed, and lifted and rolled and drove him away. Years later, someone stole the sword from a house in Massachusetts where my first four children lived with their mother; and later someone stole the Colt from an apartment in Massachusetts where I lived alone. The watch died finally, in 1980, the year my mother did.

Today is Bastille Day in 1988. Since I was a Marine captain on leave to watch with my father while he died I have lost three wives, and daily and nightly living with six children, and my left leg above the knee and most of the function of my right one. His body was as thin as mine became in 1986, struck by a car on a highway north of Boston, my life and brain and nearly all of me spared. When I came home from the hospital after seven weeks and ten operations, I saw myself in a long mirror above a chest of drawers. My son, Jeb, was pushing me in my wheelchair, down the hall to the bedroom; and I said to him: *I look like my father, the day before he died.*

Today a man named Hope phoned from Chicago to set me free with money willed by a man named MacArthur. I see my father leaving his malignant flesh, and peasants throwing over a throne my father's family served, and I know the very smallness of my needs: the house, and the hired women who keep it and me going. My father sang *la Marseillaise.* Now I see him assaulting with me the gate, the walls, the prison and armory of our flesh: my father in his final and radiant harmony, and I crippled in my chair: mere men, rushing to grace.

1988

HUSBANDS

On a sunlit December afternoon a UPS man carrying a long, wide package came up the steep hill of my driveway. The width of the package was from his armpit to his hand. I saw him through the glass door in front of my desk, and wheeled to the kitchen door and opened it, and waited for him to come up the series of six connected ramps, four of them long and parallel to each other. One ramp would be too steep; you need one inch of grade for every twelve inches you climb or descend. Turning onto the last ramp he saw me and smiled and asked how I was doing. I see a lot of UPS men. It is a simple way to shop. He had blond hair and a face reddened by the winter sun and wind, and perhaps from climbing the hill. I told him I was fine.

"That's an exercise machine," I said. "How do you feel about putting it in the bedroom?"

Whenever I ask someone to do something for me, I am

saying aloud that I cannot do it, or cannot do it well, or simply, or easily. So I very often ask with odd sentences. In the first year after my injury, with one leg gone above the knee and the other in a cast and usually hurting, I said things like *I wonder if there's any cheese* or *Does anyone want hot chocolate?* I still do.

"Sure," the UPS man said. "Where is it?"

"Down at the end of the hall."

I wheeled backward out of the kitchen to get out of his way, made a backward turn in the dining room to let him by, then followed him in the hall, and said: "All this time you've been waiting for a young wife to ask you to put it in the bedroom, and you get an old buck in a wheelchair."

Still in the hall, he said over his shoulder: "I wish my wife would do that."

"Do what?"

He was in the bedroom, and I was rolling through the door.

"Tell me to put it in the bedroom," he said.

The summer before that, I had a lap pool built in my front yard, so I could have motion out of my chair. A lap pool is three feet deep. Beside mine is a concrete slab level with my chair; from the slab, steps with aluminum railings go to the pool, and by lifting myself on the railings, I can go down and up on my butt. Most of all, the pool is to replace the beach. I love the beach, and probably will always miss it, but I cannot go there anymore without someone to pull my chair backward and tilted, so the small front wheels are above the sand. They are the ones that sink. So now, when my little girls are with me in summer, we play in the pool. My two grown sons and two friends, on payroll, built the ramp to the pool, and, at the top of my driveway, to a built-up rectangle of asphalt with railroad ties as a curb. My driveway is all steep slope, and this flat asphalt allows me to get in and out of my car.

On a beautiful early summer afternoon my son Jeb and the two friends and I were sitting on the ramp, our shirts off, when the man who delivers for the pharmacy drove up the driveway. He is a short pleasant man, retired from the gas company. He wears thick glasses, always a visored cap, and has grey hair. Reading gas meters taught him to carry dog biscuits; he says they worked better than the spray designed to fend off dogs. Always he brought biscuits for my dog, Luke, a golden retriever. Luke was lying in the shade that day, and went to the man and sat at his feet to be fed. Someone brought the bag of vitamins and medicine inside and fetched my checkbook and I paid. I see this delivery man at least every other week, yet I had forgotten his wedding anniversary. But Bill remembered, and said: "How was the fiftieth wedding anniversary?"

"Oh, it was something. They picked us up at the house in a limousine, took us to the function room. There was a hundred people there. We had cocktails, prime rib, cake, champagne, the works. I says to the wife, when you've had a car this long, it's time to trade in on a new model. She says I was thinking the same thing. I says I was thinking of trading in for two twenty-five-year-olds. She says they'd kill you."

"Fifty years," Jack said. "That's something to celebrate. Any marriage is hard."

"Oh, sure, it was hard. That first year, back in 1939, I couldn't get regular work at the shoe factory. For about six months, I couldn't get a forty-hour week. But after that it was all right."

Jeb and Jack and Bill and I looked at each other; only Bill

had a girlfriend, his fiancee. We looked back at the delivery man, reaching in his pocket for a dog biscuit.

"After the dinner and the toasts and everything, they put us in the limousine and took us home. We go upstairs and get into the bed and I says to the wife: You think we ought to try what we tried fifty years ago? She says it'll cost you money just to touch it. So next morning I go downstairs and I put a dollar bill under her orange juice glass, and I put another one under her cereal bowl, and one under her coffee cup. I put one under the sugar bowl and the salt shaker and the pepper shaker. Then I put one under my glass and bowl and cup, and one under her napkin so she'd get the message. Then I sat down and waited for her."

He stood facing us, smiling, petting Luke, putting another bone-shaped biscuit in Luke's mouth. I said: "Aren't you going to tell us the end of that story?"

"That is the end," he said, smiling, and lifted his hand in a wave, and walked away from us to his car.

On a warm blue September afternoon I went to see my paraplegic friend. A few years ago he fell off a ladder. I will call him Joe. He works for disabled people, out of an office in a nearby town on the Merrimack River. He taught me to drive with hand controls, but that is not part of his job. He did it one Sunday afternoon, at my house, saving me eight hours of lessons at ten dollars an hour.

In the parking lot outside his office, Joe was waiting in his chair. He wanted to see my new two-thousand-dollar rig: a steel box on the roof of my car that, with two chains like a bicycle's and an elongated hook, folds and lifts my chair into it, and lowers it to the ground beside my door. A button inside the car controls it. I parked beside him and opened my door and watched his face as I lowered the chair. He is a lean man with a drooping but trimmed black moustache. As the chair descended, he smiled and shook his head.

"It's too easy, Andre. It's too easy."

I had learned to drive in his Cadillac. To remove the wheels from the chair and place them and the seat cushion then the folded chair behind the driver's seat, you must sit sideways in the car, with your legs outside, so you can pull the seat as far as possible toward the steering wheel. My right knee does not bend enough for me to swing my leg in and out of a car, but in Joe's Cadillac, I could shift backward to the passenger seat and get my leg inside. In my Toyota Celica the console and handbrake are in my way, and the car's lack of depth makes this movement difficult. I said: "Nothing is too easy."

But he liked the machine. People who like machines admire its simple efficiency. People in parking lots stop to watch it work. Joe wheeled closer to the car to see the cellular phone I had bought the day before. Without a MacArthur Fellowship I would have none of this; and I would not have the car or the two-thousand-dollar wheelchair that is so much more comfortable and mobile and durable than those nine-hundred-dollar blue chairs you see in hospitals. You can go through two of them in a year, if you are active. I got the phone in case of car trouble. Joe wanted to know how the phone worked, and I showed him, and he called his office. Then we went inside and met the people working there. All but one was disabled. There was a blind man, and Joe grinned and asked him if he had read my books. The blind man laughed.

On our way out Joe introduced me to a quadriplegic, perhaps in his early forties. With him was a pretty blonde woman. Then we went through wide doors that open and close by buttons on the wall beside them, so that if you are in a chair you do not have to pull the door toward you or hold it open while you wheel across its threshold. Outside was a concrete porch and a long L-shaped ramp to the parking lot. We faced the sun and I took off my shirt and watched a black man drive a van into the parking space in front of the porch. He and Joe waved. Joe said he was from Nigeria and had a wife before his accident, a car wreck, but now she was gone. The man put his key ring between his teeth, transferred to his wheelchair on the passenger side, worked a switch there, and behind him a lift came out of the van. He wheeled onto it, worked the switch again, and came down to the asphalt. At the side of the van, he took the keys from his mouth, turned one of them in a switch, and the lift went up and back into the van, whose door closed behind it. Then he put his keys in a bag attached to the back of his chair. He wheeled to our left, to the ramp and up the first leg of it. As he turned up the last leg, facing us now, I said: "Are you having fun?"

"Oh yes; I am pumping iron."

He had a strong torso and his face was broad and young and handsome. Joe introduced us. The Nigerian was lightly sweating, and had a good handshake. I said: "I'm just starting my fourth year. How about you?"

"Six now," he said, smiling. "I love it."

"That's right," Joe said. "The crying days are over."

"And who is listening?"

He is a paraplegic. For a few minutes he and Joe talked about burning themselves, carrying hot coffee and spilling it and not knowing they were being scalded. I said: "So when my leg hurts I should think about you guys, right?"

"That's right," Joe said.

"I don't carry coffee anymore," the Nigerian said.

Then he went inside. I looked at Joe.

"You can't feel anything? From the waist down?"

"It's funny. I can feel my left nut. And look: I can move my left leg from side to side." He moved it a few times. "I can't feel it but, see, it moves. Everybody's different. One guy may be able to feel his toe. Just one of them. You know anything about the spine?"

"No."

He clenched a fist, leaving an opening in it.

"Your spine is like the fucking phone company. There's all these wires." He stuck his forefinger into the hole. "It depends on what gets cut."

"Did you see *Coming Home*?"

"That's a good movie."

"He couldn't feel her, right?"

"No."

"But you get erections."

"Voluntary, and involuntary."

"Then what?"

"It's better. Look, before you get hurt, what do you do? You get on the wife and pump away, then it's over. Now I take my time. That's why it's better. It's in the brain, Andre. Why do you want to get laid? For your brain, right?"

"I guess so. Can you have an orgasm?"

"No. It takes muscles. So what?"

"I had a problem, my first year. Making love made me think about my legs, and I couldn't come. Sometimes, but not all the time."

"So?"

"I know. But it got to me. Then in the third year, that lady you met at my house, remember her?"

"She was nice."

"She surely was. She made me feel whole again."

Behind us the door opened and the quadriplegic came out in his mechanical chair, the blonde woman behind him. They told me Nice to meet you, we all said goodbye, and Joe and I watched them go down the ramp and across the lot to his van, watched him go up a lift behind the passenger's seat, then move his chair to the steering wheel. He is able to drive with his hands. She climbed in beside him.

"Look at him," Joe said. "A quad. She's been with him for seven years, *af*ter he got fucked up. What do you think *he's* got, a seven-inch tongue?"

They drove out to the street and she waved at us. We waved and I watched her smile and hair. Then I looked at Joe.

"What," he said.

"You're telling me that you go to bed with your wife, you take your time, you get hard, your wife gets on top and does what she wants to do till she's finished, and you don't feel anything."

"That's right. And, let me tell you, there's a lot more to our marriage than sex."

That night Jack and I went to dinner at a restaurant in Haverhill with Gene and Jean Harbilas. Gene is my doctor. He and I drank vodka martinis, then we had a good bordeaux with dinner. The dinner was very good, but I had been sitting, either in the car or my chair, since leaving home early that afternoon to visit Joe, and for the last hour or so my lower back muscles ached enough to make me sweat. After dinner the young black chef came out to meet us. He was from the Gold Coast and spoke English with a French accent. He told us he had studied in Paris, and met his wife there. Someone asked what brought him to Haverhill.

"It is my wife's home," he said.

I thought how strange it was, to meet two men from Africa on the same day in the Merrimack Valley.

1990

){

Breathing

A<small>T MASSACHUSETTS GENERAL</small> Hospital, Patrick was a good nurse. He loved adrenaline, he told me; he had been a paramedic. One night when I still had my left leg, I woke to a young nurse standing above me, crying out: "Oh my God." She ran from the room. In came Patrick. Blood was spurting from an artery in my left leg. I could not see it, and I do not recall how I knew it. Two doctors came next, a black woman and a white man. But for a short time I was alone with Patrick. I told myself I was in good hands, but I did not do this with words; I surrendered myself. I focused only on breathing. I slowed my breathing, and tried to remain absolutely in the present, in each moment. I did not think. Much later, perhaps years, I remembered there was something I had not told my children, something they may be able to use. That waiting to die or to stay alive was like getting an injection as a child, when you first learned not to think, but to gather yourself into the present, to breathe slowly, to relax your muscles, even your arm as the nurse swabbed it with alcohol, to feel the cool alcohol, to smell it, to feel your feet on the floor and see the color of the wall, and nothing else as your slow breathing opened you to the incredible length and breadth and depth of one second.

1990

Part Five

BROKEN VESSELS

for Suzanne

ON THE TWENTY-THIRD of June, a Thursday afternoon in 1988, I lay on my bed and looked out the sliding glass doors at blue sky and green poplars and I wanted to die. I wanted to see You and cry out to You: *So You had three years of public life which probably weren't so bad, were probably even good most of the time, and You suffered for three days, from Gethsemane to Calvary, but You never had children taken away from You.* That is what I wanted to do when I died, but it is not why I wanted to die. I wanted to die because my little girls were in Montauk on Long Island, and had been there since Wednesday, and would be till Sunday; and I had last seen and held and heard them on Tuesday. Cadence is six, and Madeleine is seventeen months.

I wanted to die because it was summer again, and all summer and fall of 1987 I had dreaded the short light and long dark of winter, and now it was June: summer, my favorite season since boyhood, one of less clothes and more

161

hours in the sun: on the beach and the fishing boats and at Fenway Park and on the roads I used to run then walk, after twenty-five years of running; and the five-mile conditioning walks were so much more pleasurable that I was glad I lost running because of sinus headaches in my forties. It was summer again and I wanted to die because last summer I was a shut-in, but with a wife and two daughters in the house, and last August I even wrote. Then with the fall came the end of the family, so of writing; and now the long winter is over and I am shut in still, and without my children in the house; and unable to write, as I have been nearly all the days since the thirteenth of November 1987 when, five days after the girls' mother left me, she came with a court order and a kind young Haverhill police officer, and took Cadence and Madeleine away.

On Tuesday evening, the twenty-first of June in 1988, I ate pizza and Greek salad with my girls and Jack Herlihy, who lives with me, who moved into my basement in January of 1988 to help me pay the mortgage; to help me. But Wednesday and Thursday I could not eat, or hardly could, as though I were not the same man who had lived on Tuesday: in early afternoon, with my son Andre helping me, I had worked out with bench presses and chin-ups in the dining room, where Andre had carried the bench and bar and plates from the library. He rested the chinning bar on its holders on the sides of the kitchen doorway and stood behind me and helped me pull up from the wheelchair, then he pushed the chair ahead of me, and after sets of chin-ups I pulled the chair back under me with my right leg and my stump, and he held me as I lowered my body into it. This was after I had shadowboxed in my chair on the sundeck, singing with Louis Armstrong on cassette, singing for deep breathing with my stomach, and to bring joy to a sitting workout that took me most of the summer of 1987 to devise, with gratitude to my friend Jane Strüss, who taught me in voice lessons in the winter and spring of 1984 that I had spent my adult life breathing unnaturally. The shadowboxing while singing gives me the catharsis I once gained from the conditioning walks and, before those, the running that I started when I was nineteen, after celebrating or, more accurately, realizing that birthday while riding before dawn with a busload of officer candidates to the rifle range at Quantico, Virginia, during my first six weeks of Marine Corps Platoon Leaders' Class, in August of 1955.

I came home from training to my sophomore year at McNeese State College in Lake Charles, Louisiana; and to better endure the second six weeks of Platoon Leaders' Class in 1957, then active duty as an officer after college, I ran on the roads near my home for the next three years, a time in America when no one worked out, not even athletes in their off-seasons, and anyone seen running on a road had the look of either a fugitive or a man gone mad in the noonday sun. When I left the Marines in 1964 I kept running, because it — and sometimes it alone — cleared my brain and gave peace to my soul. I never exercised for longevity or to have an attractive body and, strangely, my body showed that: I always had a paunch I assumed was a beer gut until the early spring of 1987 when my right leg was still in a cast, as it was for nearly eight months, and I drank no beer, only a very occasional vodka martini my wife made me, and I could not eat more than twice a day, but with Andre's help on the weight-lifting bench I started regaining the forty or so pounds I had lost in the hospital, and my stomach spread into its old mound and I told my physical therapist, Mary Winchell, that it never was a beer gut after all. Mary came to the house three times a week and endured with me the pain of nearly every session, and the other pain that was not of the body but the spirit: that deeper and more deleterious pain that rendered me on the twenty-second and twenty-third of June 1988 not the same man at all who, after my workout on the twenty-first of June, waited for Cadence and Madeleine to come to my house.

When they did, Jack was home doing his paperwork from the Phoenix Bookstore, and he hosed water into the plastic wading pool I had given Cadence for her sixth birthday on the eleventh of June. The pool is on the sundeck, which I can be on this summer because in March David Novak and a young man named Justin built ramps from the dining room to the sunken living room, and from the living room to the sundeck. I wanted to be with Cadence, so Jack placed the feet of the wooden chaise longue in the pool and I transferred from my chair to the chaise, then lowered myself into the cold water. I was wearing gym shorts, Cadence was in her bathing suit, and I had taken off Madeleine's dress, and rubbed sun screen on her skin, and in diapers and sandals she walked smiling on the sundeck, her light brown and curly hair more blonde now in summer; but she did not want to be in the water. Sometimes she reached out for me to hold her, and I did, sitting in the pool, and I kept her feet above water till she was ready to leave again, and turned and strained in my arms, and said *Eh*, to show me she was. But she watched Cadence and me playing with a rubber Little Pony that floated, her long mane and tail trailing, and a rubber tiger that did not float, and Madeleine's small inflatable caramel-colored bear Cadence had chosen for her at The Big Apple Circus we had gone to in Boston on the fourth of June, to begin celebrating Cadence's birthday: Jack and Cadence and me in one car, and Madeleine with my grown daughter Suzanne and her friend Tom in another.

Cadence is tall and lithe, and has long red hair, and hazel eyes that show the lights of intelligence. Always she imagines the games we play. I was the Little Pony and she was the tiger; we talked for the animals, and they swam and dived to the bottom and walked on my right leg that was a coral reef, and had a picnic with iced tea on the plastic bank. There was no tea, no food. Once Madeleine's bear was bad, coming over the water to kill and eat our pony and tiger, and they dispatched him by holding a rubber beach ball on the bottom of the pool and releasing it under the floating bear, driving him up and over the side, onto the sundeck. Lynda Novak, young friend and daughter of dear friends, was with us, watching Madeleine as Cadence and I sat in the water under a blue sky, in dry but very warm air, and the sun of late June was hot and high.

I had planned to barbecue pork chops, four of them, center cut, marinating since morning in sauce in the refrigerator. When Cadence and I tired of the sun and the pool and the games in it, we went inside to watch a National Geographic documentary on sharks, a video, and while Lynda and Cadence started the movie, and Madeleine walked about, smiling and talking with her few words, and the echolalia she and usually Cadence and sometimes Lynda and I understood, I wheeled up the ramp to the dining room, and toward the kitchen, but did not get there for the chops, and the vegetables, frozen ones to give me more time with the girls. A bottle of basil had fallen from the work table my friend Bill Webb built against the rear wall of the dining room; he built it two days after Christmas because, two days before Christmas, he came to see me, and I was sitting in the dining room, in my wheelchair, and chopping turkey giblets on a small cutting board resting across my lap. *You like to cook,* he said, *and you can't do a Goddamn thing in that little kitchen of yours; you need a work bench.* The basil was on the floor, in my path; I leaned down, picked it up, flipped it into my lap as I straightened, and its top came off and basil spread and piled on my leg and stump and lap and chair.

Nothing: only some spilled basil, but Cadence was calling: *Daddy, come see the great white,* and I was confronting not basil but the weekend of 17–19 June, one of my two June weekends with Cadence and Madeleine. So I replaced the top on the jar, and with a paper towel picked up the mounds of basil, and with a sponge wiped off the rest of it. Then on the phone (*The phone is your legs,* a friend said to me once) I ordered pizza and Greek salad to be delivered, and joined my girls and Lynda in the living room to watch sharks, and Valerie Taylor of Australia testing a steel mesh shark-proof suit by letting a shark bite her arm. The pizza and salad arrived when Jack had come home from the bookstore, and he and the girls and Lynda and I ate on the sundeck.

On Friday the seventeenth of June I had had Delmonico steaks, potatoes, and snap beans. Jack was picking up the girls on his way home from the store, at about six-thirty, so at five forty-five I started scrubbing potatoes in the kitchen sink, and snapping the ends off beans and washing them. I had just finished shadowboxing on the sundeck, and I believed I could have the potatoes boiling, the beans ready, and also shower and shave before six-thirty. Too often, perhaps most days and nights, my body is still on biped time, and I wheel and reach and turn the chair to the sink or stove and twist in the chair to reach and learn yet again what my friend David Mix said last January. David lost his left leg, below the knee, to a Bouncing Betty that did not bounce, and so probably saved his life, on the first of August in 1967, while doing his work one morning as a Marine lieutenant in Vietnam. His novel, *Intricate Scars,* which I read in manuscript, is the most tenderly merciful and brutal war novel I have ever read. Last winter he said to my son Andre: *There comes a time in the life of an amputee when he realizes that everything takes three times as long.*

He was precise. That Friday night I stopped working in the kitchen long enough to shower, sitting on the stool, using Cadence's hand mirror to shave beneath and above my beard; I dried myself with a towel while sitting and lying on my bed, then wrapped my stump with two ace bandages, and pulled over it a tight stump sleeve to prevent edema. Twenty, maybe even thirty minutes, to shave and shower and shampoo and bandage and dress, yet we sat at the table for steak and boiled potatoes and snap beans and a salad of cucumbers and lettuce at nine-fifteen. And Jack was helping, from the time he got home till the meal was ready; but the kitchen is very small, and with the back of my wheelchair against the sink, I can reach the stove and nearly get food from the refrigerator to my right. I occupied all the cooking space; Jack could only set the table and be with the girls. Cadence was teaching Madeleine to see-saw in the hall, and often she called for me to come see Madeleine holding on and grinning and making sounds of delight, and I wheeled out of the kitchen and looked at the girls on the seesaw, then backed into the kitchen and time moved, as David Mix said, three times as fast as the action that once used a third of it.

Saturday's dinner was easy: I simply had to heat the potatoes and beans left over from Friday, and finish frying the steaks we had partially fried then, before we realized we had more than we needed, and the only difficulty was wheeling back and forth from the dining room table to the kitchen, holding dishes and glasses and flatware in my lap, a few at a time, then squirming and stretching in my chair to rinse them in the sink behind me, and place them in the dishwasher between the sink and refrigerator behind me. After dinner Cadence went to a dance concert with Suzanne and Tom.

I bathed Madeleine in the sink. She was happy in the bubbles from dish soap, and I hugged and dried her with a towel, and powdered her body and put a diaper on her, then buckled my seat belt around her and took her down the ramp to the living room. The late June sun was setting in the northwest, beyond the wide and high glass at the front of the house. I put her on the couch and got on it beside her, and Jack sat in a rocking chair at its foot, and we watched *Barfly* on VCR while Madeleine sat on my chest, smiling at me, pulling my beard and lower lip, her brown eyes deep, as they have been since she was a baby, when she would stare at each person who entered the house, would appear to be thinking about that man, that woman, would seem to be looking into their souls. She is my sixth child, and I have never seen a baby look at people that way. She still does.

That night on the couch she sometimes lay on my chest, her fleshy little arms hugging my neck, her soft and sweet-smelling cheek against mine. I felt her heart beating, and felt from her chest the sounds she made at my face, a series of rising and falling *oohs,* in the rhythm of soothing: *ooh*ooh*ooh*ooh.... After sunset, in the cooling room beneath the fan, she puckered her lips and smacked them in a kiss, as Suzanne had taught her, then leaned toward my face, her eyes bright, and kissed me; over and over; then she turned and reached behind her toward Jack, pointing her right hand, with its shortened forefinger. The top knuckle was severed in the sprocket of an exercise bicycle when she was a year and twenty-one days old; she has a tiny stump that Cadence says she got so that when she is older she will understand my stump. I told her to go give Jack a kiss, and lifted her to her feet and held her arms as she stepped off my chest, onto the couch, and followed it back to the arm, where Jack's arms and face waited for her: she puckered and smacked as she walked, then she kissed her godfather. During most of the movie, before she grew sleepy and I put her in the chair with me and buckled the seat belt around her and took her up the ramp and to the refrigerator for her bottle of orange juice, then to the crib and sang "Smoke Gets in Your Eyes" while hers closed, she stayed on my chest, and I held her, drew from her little body and loving heart peace and hope, and gratitude for being spared death that night on the highway, or a brain so injured it could not know and love Madeleine Elise. I said: *Madeleine, I love you;* and she smiled and said: *I luh you.*

Once I paused the movie, and lifted her from me and got onto my chair and went past the television and down the short ramp to the sundeck, and I wheeled to the front railing to piss between its posts, out in the night air, under the stars. Madeleine followed me, with Jack behind her, saying: *She's coming after you, Brother.* I turned to see her coming down the ramp, balancing well, then she glanced up and saw what I had not; and still descending, her face excited, she pointed the stump of her finger to the northwest and said: *Moon.*

I looked ahead of me and up at a new moon, then watched her coming to me, pointing, looking skyward, saying: *Moon. Moon. Moon.*

About the next day, Sunday the nineteenth, I remember very little, save that I was tired, as if the long preparing of the meal on Friday had taken from me some energy that I suspect was spiritual, and that I did not regain. Suzanne spent the afternoon with me and the girls. At five o'clock, in accordance with the court order, she took them to their mother's.

Today, the sixth of July 1988, I read chapter nine of St. Luke. Since starting to write this, I have begun each day's work by reading a chapter of the New Testament. Today I read: *"If anyone wishes to come after me let him deny himself, and take up his cross daily, and follow me."* And: *"took a little child and set him at his side, and said to them: 'Whoever receives this little child for my sake, receives me'."*

In June of 1987 I graduated from physical therapy at home with Mary Winchell: she taught me to transfer from my wheel chair to the passenger seat of a car, meaning the Visiting Nurses Association and Blue Cross and Blue Shield would no longer pay her to come work with me. But it was time: for the physical therapy clinic at Hale Hospital in Haverhill; for Judith Tranberg, called Mrs. T by herself and almost everyone who knows her: a lady who worked at Walter Reed with amputees from the Korean War, a lady whose lined, brown, merry and profound face and hazel eyes and deep tobacco voice I loved at once. On the twenty-second of July I wheeled into her clinic and said to her: *They've always told me my left leg is my best one,* and she said: *Why did they tell you your left leg is your best one?* I said: *I like you. I had my spirit till June, then the surgeon took off the cast and I saw my right leg and I started listening to my body. But now my spirit is back.* Mrs. T said: *I never listen to the body; only the spirit.*

My right leg looked like one found on a battlefield, perhaps a day after its severance from the body it had grown with. Except it was not bloated. It was very thin and the flesh had red and yellow hues and the foot was often purple and nearly always the big toe was painful. I do not know why. On the end of my stump was what people thought then was a blister, though it was a stitch which would become infected and, a year later, require surgery, a debridement. So Mrs. T told me not to use the artificial leg. She started me on parallel bars with the atrophied right leg, whose knee probably bent thirty-two degrees, and was never supposed to bend over forty-five, because of the shattered femur and the scar tissue in my thigh muscles, and the hole under my knee where a bone is now grafted. The tibia was also shattered, and part of my calf muscle is grafted to the top of my shin. Because of muscle and nerve damage, my surgeon, Fulton Kornack, and Mary Winchell told me my leg would never hold my foot in a neutral position, and it still does not: without a brace, from the sole and heel up my calf, my foot droops, and curls. But Mary never gave up on the knee, nor has Mrs. T, nor have I, and it can now bend sixty-three degrees.

The best person for a crippled man to cry with is a good female physical therapist, and the best place to do that crying is in the area where she works. One morning in August of 1987, shuffling with my right leg and the walker, with Mrs. T in front of me and her kind younger assistants, Kathy and Betty, beside me, I began to cry. Moving across the long therapy room with beds, machines, parallel bars, and exercise bicycles, I said through my weeping: *I'm not a man among men anymore and I'm not a man among women either.* Kathy and Betty gently told me I was fine. Mrs. T said nothing, backing ahead of me, watching my leg, my face, my body. We kept working. I cried and talked all the way into the small room with two beds that are actually leather-cushioned tables with a sheet and pillow on each, and the women helped me onto my table, and Mrs. T went to the end of it, to my foot, and began working on my ankle and toes and calf with her gentle strong hands. Then she looked up at me. Her voice has much peace whose resonance is her own pain she has moved through and beyond. *It's in Jeremiah,* she said. *The potter is making a pot and it cracks. So he smashes it, and makes a new vessel. You can't make a new vessel out of a broken one. It's time to find the real you.*

Her words and their images rose through my chest like a warm vapor, and in it was the man shattering clay, and me at Platoon Leaders' Class at Quantico, a boy who had never made love, not when I turned nineteen there, not when I went back for the second six weeks just before becoming twenty-one; and memories of myself after my training at Quantico, those times in my life when I had instinctively moved toward action, to stop fights, to help the injured or stricken, and I saw myself on the highway that night, and I said: *Yes. It makes sense. It started as a Marine, when I was eighteen; and it ended on a highway when I was almost fifty years old.*

In the hospital one night when I was in very bad shape, I woke from a dream. In the dream I was in the hospital at Camp Pendleton, California, and I was waiting for Major Forrest Joe Hunt, one of the best commanding officers I ever served with, to come and tell me where I must go now, and what I must do. But when I woke I was still at Camp Pendleton and the twenty-nine years since I left there to go on sea duty did not exist at all and I was a lieutenant waiting for Major Hunt. I asked the nurse if we were at Camp Pendleton and it took her a long time to bring me back to where and who I was. Some time later my old friend, Mark Costello, phoned me at the hospital; Mark and I met on the rifle range in Officers' Basic School at Quantico in 1958. I told him about the dream, and he said: *Marine Corps training is why you were on the highway that night.* I said I knew that, and he told me he had pulled a drowning man from the surf one summer at Mazatlan and that a Mexican man on the beach would not help him, would not go out in the water with him, and he said: *Civilian training is more conservative.* I had known that too, and had believed for a long time that we too easily accuse people of apathy or callousness when they do not help victims of assault or accidents or other disasters. I believe most people want to help, but are unable to because they have not been trained to act. Then, afterward, they think of what they could have done and they feel like physical or moral cowards or both. They should not. When I came home from the hospital a state trooper came to visit me; he told me that doctors, nurses, and paramedics were usually the only people who stopped at accidents. Sadly, he told me that people do stop when the state troopers are there; they want to look at the bodies. I am sure that the trooper's long experience has shown him a terrible truth about our species; and I am also sure that the doctors and nurses and paramedics who stop are not the only compassionate people who see an accident, but the only trained ones. *Don't just stand there, Lieutenant* they told us again and again at Officers' Basic School; *Do something, even if it's wrong.*

Until the summer and fall of 1987 I still believed that Marine training taught us to control our natural instincts to survive. But then, writing a long letter to a friend, night after night, I began to see the truth: the Marine Corps develops our natural instincts to risk ourselves for those we truly love, usually our families, for whom many human beings would risk or knowingly sacrifice their lives, and indeed many have. In a world whose inhabitants from their very beginning turned away from rather than toward each other, chose self over agape, war was a certainty; and soldiers learned that they could not endure war unless they loved each other. So I now believe that, among a species which has evolved more selfishly than lovingly, thus making soldiers an essential body of a society, there is this paradox: in order to fight wars, the Marine Corps develops in a recruit at Boot Camp, an officer candidate at Quantico, the instinct to surrender oneself for another; expands that instinct beyond families or mates or other beloveds to include all Marines. It is a Marine Corps tradition not to leave dead Marines on the battlefield, and Marines have died trying to retrieve those dead. This means that after his training a young Marine has, without words, taken a vow to offer his life for another Marine. Which means, sadly, that the Marine Corps, in a way limited to military action, has in general instilled more love in its members than Christian churches have in theirs. The Marine Corps does this, as all good teachers do, by drawing from a person instincts that are already present, and developing them by giving each person the confidence to believe in those instincts, to follow where they lead. A Marine crawling under fire to reach a a wounded Marine is performing a sacrament, an action whose essence is love, and the giving and receiving of grace.

The night before the day I cried with Mrs. T for the first time (I would cry many times during physical therapy that fall and winter and spring of 1987 and 1988, and she teases me about it still, her eyes bright and her grin crinkling her face), my wife took me to a movie. She sat in an aisle seat and I sat in my wheelchair beside her, with my plastic urinal on the floor beneath my chair leg that held my right foot elevated for better circulation of blood. Two young couples in their late teens sat directly in front of us. One of the boys was talking before the movie, then when it began he was still talking and he did not stop; the other three were not silent either, but he was the leader, the loud one. In my biped days, I was the one who asked or told people to be quiet. But in my chair I felt helpless, and said nothing. There was no rational cause for feeling that way. When you ask or tell people to be quiet in movies, they do not come rushing out of their seats, swinging at you. But a wheelchair is a spiritually pervasive seat. My wife asked the boy to please stop talking. He turned to her, looking over his left shoulder, and patronizingly harassed her, though without profanity. I said, *Cool it.* He looked at me as though he had not seen me till then; and maybe, indeed, he had not. Then he turned to the screen, and for the rest of the movie he and his friends were quiet.

I was not. I made no sounds, but I felt them inside of me. As the movie was ending, I breathed deeply and slowly with adrenaline, and relaxed as much as I could the muscles I meant to use. I would simply look at his eyes as he left his seat and turned toward me to walk around my chair and up the aisle. If he insulted me I would pull him down to me and punch him. During the closing credits he and his date and the other couple stood and left their row of seats. I watched him; he did not turn his eyes to mine. He stepped into the aisle and turned to me but did not face me; he looked instead at the carpet as he walked past me, then was gone. The adrenaline, the edge, went out of me, and seven demons worse than the first came in: sorrow and shame.

So next day, weeping, lying on my back on the table

while Mrs. T worked on my body, I told her the story and said: *If you confront a man from a wheelchair you're bullying him. Only a coward would hit a man in a chair.*

That is part of what I told her; I told her, too, about making love: always on my back, unable to kneel, and if I lay on my stomach I could barely move my lower body and had to keep my upper body raised with a suspended push-up. I did not tell her the true sorrow of lovemaking but I am certain that she knew: it made me remember my legs as they once were, and to feel too deeply how crippled I had become.

You can't make a new vessel out of a broken one. I can see her now as she said it, hear her voice, soft but impassioned with certainty, as her face and eyes were. *It's time to find the real you.*

I was working on a novella in August, but then in September, a beautiful blue September with red and orange and yellow leaves, I could not work on it any longer, for I knew that soon my wife would leave. So did Cadence. We played now on my bed with two small bears, Papa Bear and Sister Bear. She brought them to the bed, and their house was my lap; Cadence had just started kindergarten, and Sister Bear went to school, at a spot across the bed, and came home, where she and Papa Bear cooked dinners. They fished from my right leg, the bank of a river, and walked in the forest of my green camouflage Marine poncho liner, and climbed the pillows and the headboard that were mountains. I knew the mother bear was alive, but I did not ask where she was, and Cadence never told me.

But what did she see, in her heart that had already borne so much? Her fourth birthday was on the eleventh of June 1986, then on the twenty-third of July the car hit me and I was in the hospital for nearly two months, her mother coming to see me from one in the afternoon till eight at night every day save one when I told her to stay home and rest, and Cadence was at play school and with a sitter or friends until her mother came home tired at nine o'clock or later at night.

Her mother had waked her around one-thirty in the morning of the twenty-third, to tell her Daddy had been in an accident and her brother Jeb, my younger grown son, was taking Mommy to the hospital and Jeb's friend Nickie would spend the night with her, and she had cried with fear, or terror: that sudden and absolute change in a child's life, this one coming at night too, the worst of times, its absence of light in the sky and on trees and earth and manmade objects rendering her a prisoner of only what she could see: the lighted bedroom, the faces of her mother and brother and the young woman, and so a prisoner of her imagination that showed her too much of danger and death and night. Her four years of life forced her physically to be passive, unable to phone the hospital or friends, unable even to conceive of tomorrow and tomorrow and tomorrow, of life and healing and peace. Over a year later, on a September afternoon in the sun, she told me of the first time her mother brought her to see me, in intensive care: *The little room,* she said, *with all the machines. I kept that in mind,* she said. *You had that thing in your mouth and it was hard for me to kiss you. What was it for?* I told her it was probably to let me breathe. Then she said: *I thought you were dead till then.* And I said that surely Mommy told her I was alive; she said: *Yes. But I thought you were dead till I saw you.*

She came to the hospital for short visits with her mother, then friends took her home; I talked to her on the phone from the hospital bed, and she was only with her mother in the morning and late at night. She did not mind that my leg would be cut off; *he'll be asleep and he won't feel it,* she told a friend who was with her for an afternoon in Boston while her mother sat with me. *When Daddy comes home,* she told her mother, *I'm going to help him learn to walk.* At the hospital her mother sat with me, and watched the clock with me, for the morphine that, twenty minutes after the injection, would ease the pain. Then I was home in a rented hospital bed in the library adjacent to our bedroom, and through its wide door I looked at the double bed, a mattress and boxsprings on the floor, where Cadence and her mother slept. In the mornings Cadence woke first and I woke to her voice and face, sitting up in the bed, on the side where I used to sleep, and looking out the glass door to the sundeck, looking out at the sky, the morning; and talking. That fall and winter she often talked about the baby growing in her mother's body; and one night, when she and I were on the couch in the living room, she said: *Once upon a time there was a father and mother and a little girl and then they had a baby and everything went crazy.*

She was only four. That summer of 1986 her mother and I believed Cadence would only have to be four and worry about a baby coming into her life, perhaps believing the baby would draw her parents' love away from her, or would simply be in the way. And her mother and I believed that, because I had a Guggenheim grant from June of 1986 to June of 1987, we would simply write and pay the bills and she would teach her fiction workshop at home on Wednesday nights and I would try to recover from burning out as a teacher, then becoming so tired visiting colleges for money from January till July of 1986 that I spent a night in intensive care at Montpelier, Vermont, on the fourth of July, with what the cardiologist thought was a heart attack but was exhaustion; and we would have a child.

Madeleine grew inside of my wife as she visited the hospital, then as she cared for me at home, changing bandages as they taught her in the hospital, emptying urinals, bringing food to the hospital bed in the library, and juice and water, and holding my leg when I transferred from bed to chair to couch and back again; Madeleine growing inside of her as she soothed the pain in my body and soul, as she put the bed pan under me then cleaned me and it, and she watched with me as the Red Sox beat the Angels in the playoffs and lost to the Mets in the World Series, sacrifice enough for her, to watch baseball till late at night, pregnant and caring for a four-year-old energetic girl and a crippled man. But she sacrificed more: for some time, I don't know how much time, maybe two weeks or three, because it remains suspended in memory as an ordeal that broke us, or broke part of us anyway and made laughter more difficult, I had diarrhea, but not like any I had ever had before. It not only flowed from me without warning, but it gave me no sign at all, so that I did not even know when it flowed, and did not know after it had, and for some reason we could not smell it either. So when a game ended she would stand over me on the couch and turn my body toward hers, and look, and always I was foul, so foul that it took thirty minutes to clean me and get me from the couch to the bed, after midnight then, the pregnant woman going tired and unheld to bed with Cadence, who would wake her in the morning.

Which would begin with cleaning me, and that remained such a part of each day and night that I remember little else, and have no memory of the Red Sox losing the seventh game I watched from the couch. *They saved your life and put you back together,* she said, *and they can't cure this.* Gene Harbilas, my doctor and friend here, cured it, and that time was over, and so was something else: a long time of grace given us in the hospital and at home, a time of love near death and with crippling, a time when my body could do little but lie still and receive, and when her every act was of the spirit, for every act was one of love, even the resting at night for the next long day of driving to and from the hospital to sit there; or, later, waking with me at home, to give me all the sustenance she could. In the fall, after the diarrhea, she was large with Madeleine, and exhaustion had its hold on her and would not let her go again, would not release her merely to gestate and give birth, and nurse and love her baby. The victim of injuries like mine is not always the apparent one. All that year I knew that she and Cadence were the true victims.

Cadence cried often. On a night in January, while Andre was staying with us for the month of Madeleine's birth, having come up from New York to take care of Cadence and mostly me (yes: the bed pan: my son) Cadence began loudly crying and screaming. She was in her bedroom. I was no longer in the hospital bed but our new one in the bedroom, and they brought her there: her eyes were open but she did not act as though she were awake. She was isolate, screaming with terror, and she could not see or hear us; or, if she could, whatever we did and said was not strong enough to break what held her. Andre called Massachusetts General Hospital and spoke to a pediatrician, a woman. He told her what Cadence was doing and she asked whether Cadence had been under any stress. He said her father was hit by a car in July and was in the hospital for two months and they cut off his leg, and her mother just had a baby and Cadence had chicken pox then so she couldn't visit her mother in the hospital, where she stayed for a week because she had a cesarean. The doctor gasped. Then she told Andre it was night terrors. I do not remember what she told us to do, because nothing we did soothed Cadence; she kept crying and screaming, and I lay helpless on my back, wanting to rise, and hold her in my arms, and walk with her, and I yelled at the ceiling, the night sky above it: *You come down from that cross and give this child some peace!* Then we played the cassette of *Porgy and Bess* by Louis Armstrong and Ella Fitzgerald that she often went to sleep to, and she was quiet and she lay beside me and slept.

In late spring of 1987 Cadence talked me into her room, in my wheelchair; I had not been able to do it till then, but she encouraged and directed me through the series of movements, forward and back and short turns, then I was there, beside her bed on the floor. After that I could go in and read to her. One night, still in the spring, I went into her room, where she sat on the bed. I looked at her face just below mine and said: "I want to tell you something. You're a very brave and strong girl. Not many four-year-olds have had the kind of year you've had. Some children have to be lied to sometimes, but Mommy and I never had to lie to you."

"What do you mean?"

"We could always tell you the truth. We could tell you they were going to cut off my leg, and that the right one wouldn't be good, and you understood everything, and when you felt happy you were happy, and when you felt sad, you cried. You always let us know how you felt and what was wrong. You didn't see Mommy much for two months while I was in the hospital, and then she was gone for a week to have Madeleine and you only saw her for a couple of minutes at the hospital till the nurse saw your chicken pox and said you had to leave. Then Mommy came home with a baby sister. Most little girls don't go through all of that. All this year has been harder on you than on anybody else, and when you grow up, somebody will have to work awfully hard to make you unhappy, because you're going to be a brave, strong woman."

Tears flowed down her cheeks, but she was quiet and her eyes were shining, and her face was like a woman's receiving love and praise.

Then in the summer and early fall of 1987, we did lie to her, but she knew the truth anyway, or the part of it that gave her pain and demanded, again, resilience; and she brought to my bed only the two bears, the father and the daughter; and her days must have drained her: she woke with the fear of kindergarten and the other fear and sorrow she must have escaped only in sleep and with new children and work at kindergarten, and with familiar friends at play school, in the same way adults are absorbed long enough by certain people and actions to gain respite from some deep fear or pain at the center of their lives. I could no longer work. When the house was empty I phoned Jack at the Phoenix Bookstore and asked for his prayers and counsel and comfort, and I went to physical therapy three times a week, going there and back in a wheelchair van, three hours each session with Mrs. T, and the physical work and pain gave me relief, and I prayed for patience and strength and love, and played with Cadence and Madeleine, and waited for the end.

The girls' mother left on the eighth of November, a Sunday night; and people who love us helped me care for my girls until after dark, around six o'clock, on Friday the thirteenth, when she came with the court order and the Haverhill police officer. That afternoon Cadence and I were lying on my bed. Beside her was her pincher, a strip of grey cloth from the apron of her first Raggedy Ann doll, before she was a year old. She goes to sleep with it held in her fist, her thumb in her mouth. When she is tired or sad she holds it and sucks her thumb, or simply holds it; and she holds it too when she rides in a car or watches cartoons. She held it that afternoon after my lawyer phoned; his name is Scotty, he is an old friend, and he was surprised and sad as he told me of my wife's lawyer calling from the courthouse, to say my wife was coming for my daughters. I wheeled from the kitchen phone, down the short hall to my bedroom where Cadence and I had been playing, where for nearly a year we had played with stuffed animals. I also played the giant who lay on his back, and had lost a leg, and his right one was in a cast. The giant has a deep voice, and he loves animals. Cadence is the red-haired giant, but we usually talk about her in the third person, the animals and I, for Cadence is the hearts and voices of animals with the giant; when Madeleine could sit up and be with me, she became the baby giant, cradled in my arm. Most days in the first year Cadence brought to the games an animal with a missing or wounded limb, an animal who needed healing and our love.

Next to the bed I braked the wheelchair and moved from it to my place beside Cadence. She was sitting. I sat close to her and put my left arm around her and told her that judges were people who made sure everyone was protected by the law, even little children, and Mommy had gone to see one because she believed it was better for Cadence and Madeleine not to be with me, and Mommy was coming now with a policeman, to take her and Madeleine. I told her Mommy was not doing anything wrong, she was doing what she felt was right, like a good Momma Bear. Cadence held her pincher and looked straight ahead and was quiet. Her body was taut.

"I don't want to go in the car with them."

"Who's them, sweetie?"

"The judge and the police."

"No, darling. The judge won't be in the car. Neither will the policeman. It'll just be Mommy."

One of our animals we had played with since I came home from the hospital on the seventeenth of September 1986 is Oatmeal, a blond stuffed bear with pink ears and touches of pink on his cheeks and the top of his head and the back of his neck. On my birthday on the eleventh of August 1987, Cadence gave me shells and seaweed from the beach, and a prayer for a Japanese gingko tree she gave me with her mother, and Oatmeal. I am his voice; it is high. I am also the voice of his wife, Koala Bear; but after the marriage ended, Cadence stopped bringing Koala Bear to our games, save for one final night in December, while Madeleine was asleep and Cadence and I were playing in the dining room, and she said Oatmeal and Koala Bear were breaking up but maybe if Koala Bear had a baby they would love each other again; then she got a small bear from her room and put it with Koala Bear and Oatmeal and said they had a baby now and loved each other again. Then we watched Harry Dean Stanton as an angel in *One Magic Christmas*. After my birthday I kept Oatmeal on my bed; Cadence and I understand that he is a sign from her to me, when she is not here.

That afternoon she gazed in front of her; then quickly she moved: her face and upper body turned to me, her eyes darkly bright with grief and anger; and her arms and hands moved, one hand holding the pincher still, and she picked up Oatmeal and swung him backhanded into my lap. Then she turned away from me and was off the bed, circling its foot, and I watched the pallid right side of her face. When she turned at the bed's end and walked toward the hall, I saw her entire face, her right thumb in her mouth, the grey pincher hanging, moving with her strides; and in her eyes were tears. Her room is adjacent to mine, where I had slept with her mother, where I had watched all the seasons through the glass sliding door that faced northwest. Cadence walked past me, out my door, and into hers. She closed it.

My friend Joe Hurka and my oldest daughter Suzanne were in the house; Joe had been with us all week, driving back and forth, an hour and ten minutes each way, to his job in Peterborough, New Hampshire. I called to Cadence: "Sweetie? Do you want me in your room with you?"

I had never heard her voice from behind a door and a wall as well; always her door was open. Her voice was too old, too sorrowful for five; it was soft because she is a child, but its sound was that of a woman, suffering alone: "No."

I moved onto the wheelchair and turned it toward the door, the hall, her room. I wheeled at an angle through her doorway: she lay above me in her bunk on the left side of the room. She was on her back and sucking her right thumb and holding the pincher in her fist; she looked straight above her, and if she saw anything palpable it was the ceiling. She was pale, and tears were in her right eye, but not on her cheek. I moved to the bunk and looked up at her.

The bunk was only a few months old and, before that, she had a low bed and when she lay on it at night and I sat above her in my chair, she could not see the pictures in the books I read aloud. So we lay on my bed to read. But from the bunk she could look down over my shoulder at the pictures. She climbed a slanted wooden ladder to get on it, and I had told Mrs. T I wanted to learn to climb that ladder. *Not yet, Mr. Andre,* she had said; *not yet.* In that moment in Cadence's room, looking at her face, I said in my heart: *Fuck this cripple shit*, and I pushed the two levers that brake the wheels, and with my left hand I reached up and held the wooden side of the bunk and with my right I pushed up from the arm of the chair. I had learned from Mrs. T not to think about a new movement, but simply to do it. I rose, my extended right arm taking my weight on the padded arm of the chair, and my left trying to straighten, to lift my body up and to pivot onto the mattress beside Cadence. I called Joe and he came quickly down the hall and, standing behind me, he held me under my arms and lifted, and I was on the bunk. Cadence was sitting now, and blood colored her face; her wet eyes shone, and she was grinning.

"*Da*ddy. You got *up* here."

Joe left us, and I lay beside her, watching her face, listening to her voice raised by excitement, talking about me on the bunk. I said now we knew I could lie on the bunk at night and read to her. She crawled to the foot of the bed and faced me. Beyond her, two windows showed the grey sky in the southeast and the greyish white trunks of poplars without leaves. Cadence lowered her head and somersaulted, and her long bent legs arced above us, her feet struck the mattress, and her arms rose toward me, ahead of her face and chest. Her eyes were bright and dry, looking into mine, and she was laughing.

We were on the bunk for an hour or more. We did not talk about our sorrow, but Cadence's face paled, while Suzanne and Joe waited with Madeleine in the dining room for the car to come. When it did, Suzanne called me, and Joe came and stood behind the wheelchair and held my upper body as I moved down from the bunk. In the dining room Madeleine was in her high chair; Suzanne was feeding her cottage cheese. I talked with the young police officer, then hugged and kissed Madeleine and Cadence goodbye.

In Salem District Court I got shared but not physical custody. The girls would be with me two weekends a month, Thursday afternoons and alternate Monday afternoons through dinner, half a week during the week-long vacations from school, and two weeks in summer. *That's a lot of time,* people say. Until I tell them it is four nights a month with my two daughters, except for the two weeks in summer, and ask them if their own fathers spent only four nights a month with them when they were children (of course many say yes, or even less); or until I tell them that if I were making a living by traveling and earning a hundred thousand a year and spent only four nights a month with my family I would not be a good father. The family court system in Massachusetts appears to define a father as a sperm bank with a checkbook. But that is simply the way they make a father feel, and implicit in their dealings is an admonishment to the father to be grateful for any time at all with his children. The truth is that families are asunder, so the country is too, and no one knows what to do about this, or even why it is so. When the court receives one of these tragedies it naturally assigns the children to the mother's house, and makes the father's house a place for the children to visit. This is not fatherhood. My own view is that one house is not a home; our home has now become two houses.

On the tenth of January 1988, Madeleine was a year old. It was a Sunday, and one of my weekends with the girls, and we had balloons and a cake and small presents, and Cadence blew out the candle for her sister. During that time in winter I was still watching Cadence for signs of pain, as Suzanne and Andre and Jack were, and Marian and David Novak, and Joe Hurka and Tom. Madeleine was sometimes confused or frightened in her crib at night, but never for long. She is a happy little girl, and Cadence and Suzanne and Jack and I learned during the days of Christmas that "Silent Night" soothes her, and I sing it to her still, we all do, when she is troubled; and she stops crying. Usually she starts singing at *holy night, all is calm,* not with words but with the melody, and once this summer she sang the melody to Cadence when she was crying. We all knew that Madeleine, only ten months old when the family separated, was least touched, was the more fortunate of the children, if indeed anything about this can be fortunate for one of the children. So we watched Cadence, and let her be sad or angry, and talked with her; and we hugged and kissed Madeleine, and played with her, fed her, taught her words, and sang her to sleep.

The fifth of February was a Friday in 1988, and the first night of a weekend with the girls. Suzanne brought them into the house shortly after six o'clock in the evening; I was in the shower, sitting on the stool, and she brought them to the bathroom door to greet me. When I wheeled out of the bathroom into the dining room, a towel covering my lap, Cadence was in the living room, pedaling my exercise bicycle. A kind woman had given it to me when she saw me working on one at physical therapy, and learned from Mrs. T that I did not have the money to buy one. With my foot held by the pedal strap I could push the pedal down and pull it up, but my knee would not bend enough for me to push the wheel in a circle. In February I did not have the long ramp to the living room, against its rear wall, but a short steep one going straight down from the dining room, and I could not climb or descend it alone, because my chair would turn over. Madeleine was in the dining room, crawling, and Suzanne stood behind me, in the doorway between the dining room and kitchen, talking on the phone and looking at the girls. I was near the ramp, and Cadence was saying: *Watch this, Daddy,* and was standing on the right pedal with her right foot, stretching her left leg up behind her, holding with both hands the grip on the right end of the handlebar, and pushing the pedal around and around.

Then she was sitting on the seat and pedaling and Madeleine crawled down the ramp and toward her and the bicycle, and Cadence said: *Madeleine, no,* as Madeleine reached with her right hand to the chain guard at the wheel and her index finger went into a notch I had never seen, and a tooth of the sprocket cut her with a sound distinct among those of the moving chain and spinning wheel and Suzanne's voice: a *thunk,* followed at once by the sound of Madeleine's head striking the floor as she fell back from the pain, and screamed. She did not stop. Cadence's face was pale and frightened and ashamed, and I said: *She'll be all right, darling. Is it her head or her finger?* and Cadence said: *It's her finger and it's* bleed*ing,* and Suzanne was there, bending for Madeleine, reaching for her, saying: *It* is *her finger and it's cut* off. Three of my four daughters, and I see their faces now: the oldest bravely grieving, the youngest red with the screams that were as long as her breathing allowed, and above them the five-year-old, pale with the horror of the bleeding stump she saw and the belief that she alone was responsible.

Then Suzanne was rising with Madeleine in her arms and saying: *I have to find the finger; they can sew it back on,* and bringing Madeleine up the ramp to me. She was screaming and kicking and writhing and I held her and looked at her tiny index and middle fingers of her right hand: the top

knuckle of her index finger was severed, and so was the
inside tip of her middle finger, at an angle going up and
across her fingernail. In months, that part of her middle
finger would grow back. Suzanne told Cadence to stop the
chain because Madeleine's finger could be stuck in it, and
she dialed 911, and the police officer told her to put the
dismembered piece in ice. Cadence came up the ramp; I was
frightened of bleeding and shock, and had only a towel,
which does not stop bleeding. I said to Cadence: *Go get me
a bandana.* She turned and sprinted down the hall toward
my room, and I called after her: *In the second drawer of my
chest,* and she ran back with a clean bandana she held out
to me. Suzanne was searching the bicycle chain and the
living room, and Cadence watched me wrap Madeleine's
fingers. I held her kicking legs up but she did not go into
shock and she did not stop screaming, while Suzanne found
the rest of her finger lying on the floor, and wrapped it in
ice and put it in the refrigerator, and twice I told Cadence
it was not her fault and she must never think it was.

But she did not hear me. I imagine she heard very little
but Madeleine's screaming, and perhaps her own voice saying *Madeleine, no,* before either Suzanne or I could see what
was about to happen, an instant before that sound of the
sprocket tooth cutting through flesh and bone; and she
probably saw, besides her sister's screaming and tearful
face and bandaged bleeding hand, and the blood on Madeleine's clothes and on the towel and chair and me, her own
images: her minutes of pleasure on the bicycle before Madeleine crawled down the ramp toward her and then once
again, and so quickly again, her life became fear and pain
and sorrow, already and again demanding of her resilience
and resolve. When a police officer and two paramedics ar-

rived, she said she wanted to go in the ambulance with Madeleine and Suzanne.

By then Tom and Jack were there, and I was drying and dressing. The police officer found the small piece of Madeleine's middle finger in the chain and ran outside with it, and gave it to the paramedics before they drove to Lawrence General Hospital, because Hale Hospital has no trauma center. I asked Jack to phone David Novak, and by the time I dressed and gave the officer what he needed for his report, David was in the house. I phoned Andre at work and Jeb at home, then David and Tom and Jack and I drove in David's Bronco to the hospital, twenty-five minutes away. I had put into my knapsack what I would need to spend the night in the hospital with Madeleine. Her mother was in Vermont, to ski. But in the car, talking to David, I knew that Cadence would need me more.

In the ambulance Madeleine stopped screaming, and began the sounds she made that winter when she was near sleep: *ah* ah *ah* ah ... At the hospital she cried steadily, because of the pain, but now she was afraid too and that was in her voice, even more than pain. A nurse gave her to me and I held her cheek to mine and sang "Silent Night," then Jeb was there. At Lawrence General they could not work on Madeleine's finger; they phoned Massachusetts General Hospital in Boston, then took her there. Suzanne rode with her, and Jeb and Tom followed. Suzanne dealt with the surgeons and, on the phone, reported to me; I talked to the girls' mother in Vermont; and Suzanne and Jeb and Tom stayed at the hospital until the operation was over, and Madeleine was asleep in bed. The surgeon could not sew on the part of Madeleine's finger, because of the angle of its amputation. Early next morning her mother drove to the hospital and brought her to my house; her hand was bandaged and she felt no pain; her mother had asked on the phone in Vermont if she could spend the weekend with Madeleine, and Cadence went with them for the afternoon, then in the evening her mother brought her back to me for the rest of the weekend.

When David and Jack and Cadence and I got home from Lawrence General, I put Cadence on my lap and wheeled to my bedroom and lifted her to my bed. She lay on her back and held her pincher and sucked her thumb. She watched me as I told her she had been very good when Madeleine was hurt, that she had not panicked; she asked me what that meant, and I told her, and said that some children and some grown-ups would not have been able to help Suzanne and me, and that would be very normal for a child, but I only had to tell her to get me a bandana and she had run down the hall to the drawer in my chest before I could even tell her which drawer to look in. She turned to me: "I heard you when I was running down the hall. You said the second drawer, but I already knew and I was running to it."

I told her that was true courage, that to be brave you had to be afraid, and I was very proud of her, and of Suzanne, because we were all afraid and everyone controlled it and did what had to be done. She said: "*You* were afraid?"

"Yes. That's why I was crying."

She looked at the ceiling as I told her she must never blame herself for Madeleine's finger, that no one had seen the notch in the chain guard, the bicycle had looked safe, and she had tried to stop Madeleine, had said *Madeleine, no*, and two grown-ups were right there watching and it happened too fast for anyone to stop it. She looked at me: "I started pedaling backwards when I saw her reaching for the wheel."

Then she looked up again, and I said she had done all she could to keep Madeleine from getting hurt, and it was very important for her never to feel responsible, never to blame herself, because that could hurt her soul, and its growth; and if she ever felt that way she must tell me or Mommy or Suzanne or Andre or Jeb. Her thumb was in her mouth and her pincher lay across her fingers, so part of it was at her nose, giving her the scent she loves. Finally I said: "Is there anything you want to ask me?"

Still gazing straight up, she lowered her thumb and said: "I only have one question. Why does it always happen to me? First you got hurt. Now Madeleine is hurt. Maybe next Mommy will get hurt. Or I will."

I closed my eyes and waited for images, for words, but no words rose from my heart; I saw only Cadence's face for over a year and a half now, suffering and enduring and claiming and claiming cheer and joy and harmony with her body and spirit, and so with her life, a child's life with so very few choices. I opened my eyes.

"I don't know," I said. "But you're getting awfully good at it."

It is what she would tell me now; or encourage me to do.

Today is the twenty-ninth of August 1988, and since the twenty-third of June, the second of two days when I wanted to die, I have not wanted my earthly life to end, have not wanted to confront You with anger and despair. I receive You in the Eucharist at daily Mass, and look at You on the cross, but mostly I watch the priest, and the old deacon, a widower, who brings me the Eucharist; and the people who walk past me to receive; and I know they have all endured their own agony, and prevailed in their own way, though not alone but drawing their hope and strength from those they love, those who love them; and from You, in the sometimes tactile, sometimes incomprehensible, sometimes seemingly lethal way that You give.

A week ago I read again *The Old Man and the Sea*, and learned from it that, above all, our bodies exist to perform the condition of our spirits: our choices, our desires, our loves. My physical mobility and my little girls have been taken from me; but I remain. So my crippling is a daily and living sculpture of certain truths: we receive and we lose, and we must try to achieve gratitude; and with that gratitude to embrace with whole hearts whatever of life that remains after the losses. No one can do this alone, for being absolutely alone finally means a life not only without people or God or both to love, but without love itself. In *The Old Man and the Sea*, Santiago is a widower and a man who prays; but the love that fills and sustains him is of life itself: living creatures, and the sky, and the sea. Without that love, he would be an old man alone in a boat.

One Sunday afternoon in July, Cadence asked Jack to bring up my reserve wheelchair from the basement, and she sat in it and wheeled about the house, and moved from it onto my bed then back to the chair, with her legs held straight, as I hold my right one when getting on and off the bed. She wheeled through the narrow bathroom door and got onto the toilet, her legs straight, her feet above the floor, and pushed her pants down; and when she pulled them up again she said it was hard to do, sitting down. She went down and up the ramp to the living room, and the one to the sundeck. *Now I know what it's like to be you,* she said. When she was ready to watch a VCR cartoon, she got onto the living room couch as I do, then pushed her chair away to make room for mine, and I moved onto the couch and she sat on my stump and nestled against my chest; and Madeleine came, walking, her arms reaching for me, and I lifted her and sat her between my leg and stump, and with both arms I held my girls.

1988/1989

ABOUT THE AUTHOR

Andre Dubus was born in Lake Charles, Louisiana, and now lives in Haverhill, Massachusetts. He has been a Marine Corps captain, a college teacher, a Guggenheim Fellow, and a member of the Iowa Writer's Workshop. He received a MacArthur Fellowship in 1988. *Broken Vessels* is his ninth book.

A NOTE ON THE TYPE

This book was set in a digitized version of Janson, a typeface long thought to have been made by the Dutchman Anton Janson, who was a practicing type founder in Leipzig during the years 1668–1687. However, it has been conclusively demonstrated that these types are actually the work of Nicholas Kis (1650–1702), a Hungarian, who most probably learned his trade from the master Dutch type founder Dirk Voskens. The type is an excellent example of the influential and sturdy Dutch types that prevailed in England up to the time William Caslon (1692–1766) developed his own incomparable designs from them.

Composed by ComCom, Division of
The Haddon Craftsmen, Allentown, Pennsylvania
Printed and bound by
Maple-Vail Book Manufacturing Group,
Binghamton, New York
Designed by Lucinda Hitchcock